DO
NOT
LIVE
AFRAID

DO
NOT
LIVE
AFRAID

**faith
in a
fearful
world**

JOHN INDERMARK

UPPER
ROOM BOOKS®
NASHVILLE

No part of this book may be used or reproduced in any manner whatsoever without permission except in the case of brief quotations embodied in critical articles or reviews. For information, write Upper Room Books, 1908 Grand Ave., Nashville, Tennessee 37212.

UPPER ROOM®, UPPER ROOM BOOKS®, and design logos are trademarks owned by The Upper Room®, a ministry of GBOD®, Nashville, Tennessee. All rights reserved.

The Upper Room Web Site: http://www.upperroom.org

Scripture quotations not otherwise identified are from the New Revised Standard Version of the Bible, © 1989 by the Division of Christian Education of the National Council of the Churches of Christ in the USA. Used by permission. All rights reserved.

Scripture quotations identified as AP are the author's paraphrase.

Cover design: Bruce Gore/Gore Studio
Cover photo: Getty Images; photo by Keith Goldstein
First printing: 2009

Library of Congress Cataloging-in-Publication

Indermark, John, 1950–
Do not live afraid : faith in a fearful world / by John Indermark.
     p. cm.
   Includes bibliographical references and index.
   ISBN 978-0-8358-9996-3 (alk. paper)
   1. Spiritual life—Christianity. 2. Fear—Religious aspects—Christianity.
I. Title.
   BV4908.5.I53 2009
   248.8'6—dc22   2009001791

Printed in the United States of America

to my late uncles

Henry Cohen   William Shovell
"Uncle Henry"   "Uncle Bill"

Career public servants

who did not fear to risk the sacrifice of self

for the greater good of the nation they loved

Other Books by
John Indermark

Gospeled Lives: Encounters with Jesus (#9971)

Hope: Our Longing for Home (#9921)

Parables and Passion: Jesus' Stories for the Days of Lent (#1005)

Traveling the Prayer Paths of Jesus (#9857)

Neglected Voices: Biblical Spirituality in the Margins (#891)

Setting the Christmas Stage: Readings for the Advent Season (#947)

Genesis of Grace: A Lenten Book of Days (#843)

To order, call customer service:

800-972-0433

or go online to The Upper Room bookstore:

www.upperroom.org

contents

acknowledgments

Do Not Live Afraid is, to be sure, easier said than done. While this book explores the why and wherefores of its doing from scriptural groundings, I owe a debt of gratitude to two men whose lives form for me yet another "script" of what it means not to live afraid. They are the two to whom I dedicate this book, one my uncle by birth and another my uncle by marriage.

Uncle Henry served as a career agent in the Secret Service once he was discharged from the Army following World War II. He never boasted of his work, in fact barely spoke of it. But from his early years as an agent investigating counterfeiting in the Chicago area to his serving on the presidential campaign detail of Richard Nixon to the completion of his work in the Washington D.C. office, my uncle stepped forward in service that figuratively and at times literally put his life on the line. He did not live afraid.

Uncle Bill followed a similar path. After serving in the Second World War, Bill enrolled in college—and even before graduating became immersed in Minnesota politics. Family folklore tells the story of Bill and another Minnesota politician flipping a coin to decide who would run for a major statewide office and who would serve as campaign manager. Bill lost that coin toss and became the campaign manager for Fritz Mondale. Bill was not afraid to set aside his personal ambitions to serve the wider good. He continued to do that, whether in his service in the Minnesota legislature and later the White House staff, or in his dogged work on behalf of incarcerated youth in a time when they had few advocates or in support of Job Corps programs at a time of looming cutbacks. Bill did not live afraid. As you read this book, I hope the qualities of living without fear will find such exemplars in your life as I have in these two men.

I am deeply indebted to the good folk at Upper Room Books for their acceptance of this project and their shepherding of it through the publication process. Robin Pippin, Editorial Director at Upper Room Books, has been a strong advocate for my writing. I am blessed with editors there, such as Rita Collett for thorough copy editing and Denise Duke for handling matters of verification. To them and the administrative staff at Upper Room Books, with whom I have worked over the years, particularly Joane Pettus and Karen Duncan, I am grateful for all their good work.

Early readers of portions of this manuscript have also included the cadre of writers I have met with on a monthly basis for years. Jenelle Varila, Brian Harrison, Bryan Penttila, Lorne Wirkkala: wordsmiths all and friends as well. Thank you. And to my wife and partner, Judy, for tireless support of my writing, occasional fearless critique when it does not read well, and for sharing this journey with love: my love and appreciation always.

Finally, this book was just taking shape when Uncle Bill's health began to fail. But Bill strongly encouraged me to carry through on this theme. From his own experience in American politics, he lamented the power of fear exercised all too often, especially in recent perverse manipulations of the body politic for partisan ends. So while he did not live to see this book's completion, I hope that some of his spirit carries through these words. Thanks, Bill!

using this book

FEAR IS A GREAT MOTIVATOR, but it is not a saving one. Fear can generate many things, but it cannot generate the gospel's core: love. First John 4:18a is not engaging in sophistry when it says, "There is no fear in love." It is telling the truth about Christian discipleship. It is telling the truth to purveyors and provocateurs of fear, whether inside or outside the church. Fear relies on the threat of death in relationship, spirit, or body. The gospel of Jesus Christ relies on fear's nullification: God's gracious promise of life.

With remarkable frequency, the first word God speaks to individuals and groups poised at the edge of momentous decision or holy encounter is this: "Do not be afraid. Do not fear." What is intended goes beyond an attitude adjustment on our part. What is intended are lives empowered by that decisive word, so that "do not be afraid" finds its fullest expression when we do not live afraid. Faith does not call us merely to live without fear inside the sanctuary. Discipleship calls us to confront appeals to fear in the world around us and to live our lives and bear our witness accordingly. This book invites you to take that word to heart and beyond heart—to living. It will be a challenge, for we live in fearful times, confronted by cultures, even theologies, that promote fear.

Look at the contents page if you have not done so already. The first section of this book is titled "Framing the Call." The two chapters in this section lay out the underlying framework of this book's invitation not to live afraid. The first chapter explores traditions related to the "fear of God" in the biblical witness. Chapter 2 then considers promises that serve as foundations for a life lived beyond fear: God's presence, favor, and advocacy.

The second section of the book consists of five chapters. Each chapter considers a single theme that explores what God's message of "do no be afraid" makes possible in our lives: trust, vocation, witness, justice, and transformation. Each chapter uses passages from the Hebrew and Christian scriptures as starting points for delving into those themes. Please read the passages listed below the chapter title before reading the chapter itself.

Every chapter ends with suggestions for four spiritual exercises. Do not try to do all four the same day you read the chapter. Ideally, read the chapter one day, then do one exercise each day following. Since the exercises grow out of issues raised within the chapter, you may find the exercises leading you to review and reread the chapter. If you read this book while taking part in a group study, the weekly rhythm will consist of five days of reading and exercises, a sixth day for the group gathering, and a seventh day for sabbath reflection before entering the next chapter.

The third section of the book is an appendix that includes suggestions for group sessions. If you will be taking part in the leadership of such a group, note that one part of the appendix offers a "template" for the sessions printed on facing pages for easier copying. It provides the basic outline to be followed each week. The individual session plans that follow do not repeat that outline but rather offer specific activities or discussions for several of its elements.

"The Practice of Faith in a Fearful World" is the subtitle of this book and is a fitting word with which to enter into its reading. For in the end, the aim of this book is not an academic exercise in the definition of fear. Its aim is to encourage you to practice faith that does not live afraid. I offer it in the hope that you will find in the promises of God and in the experience of love received and offered, the means to live by trust and not fear as a disciple of Jesus Christ.

PART I

framing the call

1

Fear and Faith

EXODUS 1:8-21
PROVERBS 9:10
1 JOHN 4:18-19

The fear of the LORD is the beginning of wisdom
. . . .
There is no fear in love.

IF THE TWO QUOTES above represented two sides of a continuum, at which end would you find yourself most at home? Or would you fall somewhere in the middle? My Old Testament professor in seminary sometimes spoke of texts that seemingly disagree or are contradictory as being "in dialogue with one another." The two lines above certainly qualify as partners in such a conversation. Each contains a truth, an important truth, but not the whole truth. So in the dialogue between those two lines, what might your voice and experience add to that exchange?

From the title of this book you might surmise that I lean strongly in the direction of love's trumping fear. That is true—to a point. Love removes fear as the totality of our relationship with God. Love provides the basis for our trust in God and the model for our engagement with the world. The world has more than its share of political and social—and yes, regrettably, religious—fear mongers who manipulate alarm as a tool to coerce uncritical loyalty and squelch opposition.

Does that mean this quote from Proverbs and all those many, many other passages in scripture that speak positively of "the fear of the LORD" belong to an antiquated religion of superstition not fit for modern or postmodern sensibilities? No. Those texts bring a needed perspective. So how can we balance fear as the beginning of wisdom with love casting out fear? And how can we do so in such a way that encourages us not to live afraid? For that we begin with Shiphrah and Puah.

The Midwives' Tale

One common trigger of fear resides in an imbalance of power between individuals or groups. Those on the short end of the stick fear the ability of those in control to use power against them. Sometimes that fear arises out of a general sense of dread, the mere possibility that power may be abused. Far too often, such fear arises out of actual experience. The silence of abused children may be evoked—or enforced—by all-too-real harm at the hands of formerly trusted adults. The murders of civil rights workers in Mississippi in 1964 or the targeting of dissidents in Iraq, prewar and postwar, illustrate fear's ultimate card: the power to inflict death. Fear relies on the threat of extinction to control the lives of others.

Such stories of fear have ancient roots. One of the foundational narratives for Judaism and Christianity recounts such a story. It begins with a pharaoh who no longer knew Joseph. His lack of memory led to the increasingly brutal treatment of Joseph's people, now called the "Hebrews" rather than the Israelites.

Hebrews is a curious word. It originated not as an ethnic or religious designation but a term of social class in the ancient Near East. Hebrews could refer to any marginalized group that had little or no standing in society. Pharaoh's categorizing the Israelites as "Hebrews" underscored disparity of power and a legitimate cause to fear. These "nobodies" in Egypt found themselves targeted by arguably the most absolute of all rulers in this era. This particular pharaoh used that unqualified dominance to enslave the Hebrews. Beyond that, this pharaoh employed a scheme of systematic elimination of male Hebrew children, an ingenious plan. Without male children, future generations born would all have Egyptian fathers. It was to be, if you will, genocide by premeditated generational rape. But the genocide would not take place. The fear generated by Pharaoh's power met its match in another fear.

"But the midwives feared God." Maybe the story would sound more presentable to modern ears if "trusted" or "loved" or "followed" had been used in place of "feared" in that verse. But there it is, bright as day, with no textual variant in the manuscripts to suggest an alternate meaning. The midwives *feared* God. Does that mean Shiphrah and Puah lived afraid? Quite the contrary. For them to live in fear would have meant caving in to the more immediate threat of death that Pharaoh could easily inflict. To live in fear would have resulted in the midwives seeking the path of least resistance lest they suffer the consequences of Pharaoh's oppressive rule. To live in fear would have given in to "do as you're told and you will live to see another day." Instead, Shiphrah and Puah do not do what they're told by Pharaoh. They do not live in fear but in faith. As a result, not only do the targeted children live, but Shiphrah and Puah live to see another day, a day that eventually brings them children of their own.

If it were not for the deadly purposes at work here, the midwives' tale borders on the comic. The unswerving will of the incarnate deity credited with commanding the Nile is swerved 180 degrees by two slave women. The all-powerful word of Pharaoh to levy death is rendered momentarily impotent by the admittedly deceitful words of midwives who hide their actions for the sake of saving more children. By story's end, Pharaoh still holds the Hebrews in bondage. But the ending reveals that the fear of Pharaoh, whose power inflicts captivity and death, cannot withstand the fear of God, whose power brings freedom and raises life.

The Fear of God

So what exactly does the biblical witness mean by "the fear of God," whether for the Hebrew midwives or in the many other contexts of its use in scripture? Scholars identify two key elements of the "fear of God" in the Bible. The first has to do with holy encounter that produces awe in the face of mystery. The second has to do with a moral or ethical priority that results from seeing divine purpose in the doing of what is good, just, and compassionate. How do these biblical perspectives impact our present experience of God and what it means not to live afraid?

Some practices of worship and spirituality tend to transport encounter with the Holy One from the realm of awe into the sphere of the casual. I do not mean this as a value judgment about dress codes, as in whether the minister wears a pulpit robe or street gear into the sanctuary. This casualness bears more on the attitude we bring or the atmosphere we foster as we seek holy encounter. I understand the need to make the church less off-putting to seekers who did not grow up within the "system." Heaven knows we need more welcoming and hospitable faith communities. But in our efforts to make religion more accessible and to demystify it for ease of approach, have we sold the birthright of religious awe for a domesticated pottage of God-as-our-chum? You can't guarantee or produce such awe by advertising that Starbucks will be served at the coffee hour by friendly hosts. Awe is encounter with Mystery.

In C. S. Lewis's fantasy *The Lion, the Witch, and the Wardrobe*, a lion named Aslan serves as its Christ-figure. Near the end of the book, the characters named Tumnus and Lucy exchange these words about Aslan.

Tumnus: You musn't press him. After all, he's not a tame lion.
Lucy: No. But he is good.

The point Lewis makes about Aslan is a fitting metaphor for God. Like Aslan, God is not "tame" in spite of our occasional best efforts to make God so. The goodness of God does not eliminate

DO NOT LIVE AFRAID

that untamed nature of God. Rather, that goodness helps explain why we would draw closer to One whose presence may still evoke awe that borders on fear. Such awe moved Moses to take off his shoes because he was standing on holy ground. Such awe collapsed Peter at the feet of Jesus after a miraculous catch of fish. Such awe may come whenever and wherever we find ourselves standing in the presence of Mystery that overwhelms us.

One dictionary speaks of awe as "an emotion of mingled reverence, dread, and wonder." Of course, we do not speak of awe as much as we experience it. Some people partake of awe when seeing a new life delivered into this world, an infant who is wondrously part of them and yet at the same time entirely new and other. Many others experience awe in some inexpressible encounter in the natural world: standing for the first time at the edge of the Grand Canyon; floating on clear water while a sea turtle glides silently beneath them; standing inside an ice cave with the sun shining every shade of blue possible in the ice above and around. And sometimes, graciously, mysteriously, such encounters of awe remind us and even convey to us the presence of God.

There is a thin line between awe and fear as that earlier dictionary definition implies. You have good reason to fear while peering over the edge of the Grand Canyon. Yet many feel drawn to such places because of the possibility for wonder. Likewise, some biblical stories whisper there is cause to fear in the wondrous presence of God. The ark of the covenant shifts while being carried; a man called Uzzah lifts up his hand to steady it, and in touching it he dies. Second Samuel 6:9 ominously but understandingly adds at that point: "David was afraid of the LORD that day." An even more ancient story tells of Jacob referring to God as the "Fear of Isaac." God as the "Fear"? Such stories raise far more questions than they answer. But they underscore a critical truth in spiritual life: God is Other than us. To encounter God is to stand and sometimes tremble on holy ground with awe and wonder. God is the untamed One—yet God is also the good One.

The Fear of God and Ethics

God's goodness moves us to the second function of the fear of God in the biblical witness. Fear linked to the God who is good forms an initial motivation for us to do what is right, just, and compassionate. Fear linked to the God who is good provides an initial disinclination for us that leads to avoiding what is wrong and oppressive and hard-hearted. This chapter's opening quote from Proverbs about the fear of God as the beginning of wisdom hints in that direction. In the book of Proverbs, wisdom chiefly concerns itself with doing what is right and avoiding what is evil. But the book of Proverbs is not the only biblical text where the moral and ethical imperative of the fear of God goes named. Listen to the reasoning, albeit shaky, behind Abraham's attempt to pass off his wife Sarah as his sister when he entered the land of King Abimelech: "I did it because I thought, There is no fear of God at all in this place, and they will kill me because of my wife" (Gen. 20:11). The book of Leviticus prohibited defrauding one's neighbor or profiting from the vulnerabilities of strangers based on injunctions to fear God. Biblically speaking, the fear of God intends good to be done precisely because God is good.

But what might the fear of God have to do with contemporary moral and ethical imperatives? A modern proverb, often attributed to the great nineteenth-century Russian writer Fyodor Dostoevsky, states: "If there is no God, everything is permissible." Some argue, and with unfortunately solid historical evidence, that some of history's most horrific violence has been done in the name of God. Violence in the name of God may be the ultimate taking of God's name in vain. But consider the equally chilling import of the word attributed to Dostoevsky. If there is no God, if nothing beyond the horizon of this life calls this world's powers into account for what happens between the birth and death of any individual or institution, what happens then? I would answer: the killing fields of Cambodia, the ovens of Auschwitz, the treacheries in Darfur, and all the grim actions unchecked by any fear of authority beyond the limits of what can be done.

The ethic of "everything is permissible" needs not wait on such obscene examples to be witnessed. Day in and day out, "everything is permissible" allows individual acts of greed or vindictiveness, prejudice or hatred, to proceed unchecked. Conscience may inhibit such behavior. But some are more conscientious than others, and some are more self-disciplined in the exercise of restraint by conscience than others. In the meantime, the times become mean without something larger than individual conscience to temper them. Social structures may restrain. But what happens when the society and those who set its rules abuse and oppress? The fear of God as the beginning of ethical wisdom does not teach that we must cower before an all-powerful being out of fear lest we be snuffed out of existence. The fear of God in terms of ethics teaches that accountability does not end on the claims of self-interest or "what I (we) think I (we) can get away with." Even more decisively for individuals and communities of faith, the fear of God strips away the claims of lesser powers that urge us to stand in fear of them. The divine and supreme Pharaoh could cajole and threaten the midwives all he wanted. The bottom line was that Shiphrah and Puah understood that the kind of fear Pharaoh thrived upon had a mortal weakness. The kind of fear that powers and institutions would use in our day to harass and herd and dehumanize us possesses that same weakness. They are not God. They may have the power to inflict death, but they do not have the power to restore life. That is the story of the midwives. That is the story of Easter.

The midwives' refusal to fear Pharaoh because they fear God leads to a key ethical consideration. *Fear: A Cultural History* examines a variety of fears and anxieties in Britain and the United States over the past two centuries. In its preface, author Joanna Bourke reflects on more recent experiences of fear in response to terror and "wars on terror." Among those reflections, she writes:

The routine portrayal of violent death in the mass media has blunted sensibilities: when hearing about real-life viciousness we may feel pity or distaste, but when we identify the emotion of fear it is our fear that concerns us. It is the fear *of* something that may befall us, rather than fear *for* others. . . . It is time we returned to a politics which feared *for* the lives of others, near and far.[1]

The distinction is key: fear *of* others (or something) versus fear *for* others. Far too often, we obsess over what or whom we are afraid *of*. All of us could submit a long list here. But the more pressing ethical concern is this: whom are we afraid *for*. That is, whose vulnerability or need cries out not only for our recognition but our response? The biblical witness in general and the ministry of Jesus in particular push us in that direction. Fear of the Samaritans became supplanted by fear for the neighbor we encounter in need. Fear of the Gentiles tainting the purity of the church was overwhelmed by fear for a body in Christ called to be one. The fear of God as the beginning of wisdom summons our fearing for the stranger rather than our lashing out in fear of those who are different.

Fear, Faith, and Not Living Afraid

The fear of God begins wisdom . . . but does wisdom end there? Can we reduce the totality of our knowledge and experience of God to fear? Consider the relationships that bring the grace of unconditional love into your experience. Does fear drive such love or result in such grace for you? It does not in my life. I would be surprised—I would be afraid!—if it did in yours.

The fear of God expresses the mystery of encounter with God. The fear of God serves as metaphor for the motivation of moral and ethical judgments that do not reduce to "might makes right." But in those encounters, and through those ethics that bind us in covenant with neighbors and strangers, we come to experience

God as the One who then gives us cause to "fear not." For all the reasons amplified before, this book does not deny that the fear of God is the beginning of wisdom. But for all the reasons we shall soon take up, this book will affirm that the very experience of God in our lives makes it possible and even necessary to move from fear toward love. This deepening wisdom does not abandon the experience of awe or the summons of ethics. If anything, this wisdom brings them into sharper relief as we grow in relationship with God and in community with the whole of God's people and creation.

God is the one who encourages us in this movement from wisdom's beginning in fear to wisdom's fulfillment in love. This movement does not await the closing of the Hebrew scriptures' curtain and the raising of the good news. We discover the cause and call to "fear not" already present in God's working among the people of Israel.

Why is fear not the final word? How might the life of faith enable us not to live afraid before God and in the face of this world? For that, we have the assurance of a prophet named Isaiah to Jewish exiles in Babylon. For that, we have the testimony of another visionary who offered revelations to the Christian community persecuted by Roman imperial power. Both affirm we need not live afraid based on three promises:

God's presence. . .

God's favor. . .

and God's advocacy revealed in saving activities.

SPIRITUAL EXERCISE #1

Recall an experience when you felt a sense of awe.

- What evoked that feeling, and why?
- How has that experience changed you?

Consider a spiritual experience that generated awe in you. (This could be the same experience recalled above.)

- How did you sense mystery or the holy in that experience?
- How has that encounter formed your understanding and practice of faith?

Holy God, open me to your presence, open me to your purpose, open me to you.

SPIRITUAL EXERCISE #2

Spend this day (or the next, if you do this at night) watching and listening for ways in which fear is appealed to, referenced, or embodied in conversations, in relationships, in the media.

- What threats underlie each of those fears?
- What responses on our part does that fear result in or seek to evoke?

Hold those fears up to the light of this chapter and your reflection on it.

- What word does faith speak to those fears?
- What action or response does faith evoke in the face of such fears?

SPIRITUAL EXERCISE #3

Reread the quote from Joanna Bourke on page 21 and the paragraph following.

- For whom in your community do you fear?
- What are they at risk of or threatened by?

Consider a specific action you can take on behalf of those for whom you fear.

- Commit to taking that action this day, if possible, or within the next week.
- Pray for the Spirit's leading in your act and God's grace to watch over those for whom you act.

SPIRITUAL EXERCISE #4

Speak aloud this line from the song "Amazing Grace":

'Twas grace that taught my heart to fear, and grace my fears relieved.

Journal your thoughts in response to this question: In what ways do those words reflect your experience of God?

Use this hymn line as a litany for personal prayer.

- Offer it aloud, then in silence pray what comes to your heart.
- Continue the litany as long as you feel led to pray with these words.

2

God's Presence, Favor, and Advocacy

ISAIAH 41:10
REVELATION 21:3-4

I GREW UP LOVING old Westerns. TV shows, movies; it didn't really matter. Hopalong Cassidy. John Wayne. *Wanted: Dead or Alive. High Noon*. You name it. I probably watched it.

One of the myths of the Old West popularized in many of these dramas is the rugged individual who stands alone. Deserted by townspeople, left by romantic interests and comic-relief sidekicks, the hero shows no fear as he (and with few exceptions the portrayals are "he") and he alone faces down the ruthless cutthroat or conniving gangs. Such dramas leave the impression that courage remains an ultimately solitary exercise of setting fear aside.

Courage can take that form on occasion. The image of the young man who stood alone in front of a tank in Tiananmen Square comes to mind. But lonely heroic stands do not exhaust the possibilities for living without fear. A more frequent emphasis from the biblical stories suggest those lonely stands are the exception. Living without fear more often than not requires community. Standing strong becomes easier with the knowledge and gift of others who stand with you and for you. The ability to find in another the courage to stand and set fear aside provides the basis for the Bible's constantly pointing us toward the promises of God.

Why? The promises of God bring to us and to all creation the affirmation that we are not in this endeavor alone, unaided, uncared for. We do not have to stand alone. We have others, and above all we have One, upon whom we may lean for support and strength. Leaning is not necessarily a stance that immediately precedes falling. Leaning can be a posture that puts us into contact with some thing, some One, that braces us when we might otherwise fall. God is one upon whom we may lean in the face of fear. The promises to which we now turn form a threefold foundation for not living afraid. They are promises to which both Isaiah and Revelation bear witness: God's presence, favor, and advocacy.

Holy Presence

For Jewish exiles in the imperial capital of Babylon, for the seer John exiled to the tiny island of Patmos by the imperial power of Rome, God's presence did not come as an easily made assumption. Absence, more than presence, could easily have been felt as the dominant experience: absence from home, absence from a beloved land and community, absence imposed by oppressive regimes that routinely relied upon fear as the way to get things done. Yet in such settings, the authors of Isaiah 41 and Revelation 21 issued to their communities radical promises of God's presence.

Both Isaiah and Revelation offer these promises in the present tense. "Do not fear, for I *am* with you. . . . See, the home of God *is* among mortals" (emphasis added). Both authors and passages go on to assert future blessings of God, but the foundational promise is that God is with us—now, here. Remember that these affirmations do not come from seats of powers or comfortable sanctuaries where all is well and God's presence can be easily presumed.

Isaiah 41 speaks out of—and into—the experience of exile. Home and land lay hundreds of miles and decades of servitude away. For some, the more credible assertion would have been God's absence. And there is a place and time for lament, as Job and many of the Psalms make clear. But to a fractured community who may have felt bereft of, if not outright abandoned by, God's holy presence, Isaiah 41 asserts that God *is* here. The word of Revelation came in no less strenuous a time. The church suffered persecution by Rome, most likely during the time of the emperor Domitian. The exile of Revelation's author to Patmos attempted to squelch the church's leadership and thus its vitality. Yet circumstances that might have foretold God's withdrawal from the scene became instead the setting for this climactic vision that God is with God's people now. In the midst of persecution, in the face of death, God's home *is* among mortals.

The defiant declaration of God's presence in such times to bring encouragement to live without fear asserts great promise but requires great faith—even today. For now as then, the presence of God may not always and everywhere be an easy assumption to make. God's presence may not roll off the tongue lightly for parents in developing countries who watch their children die from diseases largely banished from industrialized nations. God's presence may not be an easy presumption of families in industrialized nations who cannot afford health insurance or care that is readily available to those able to pay the price. The presence of God may seem distant to those who can be held without charges and interrogated by methods most parts of the civilized world denounce as torture. The presence of God may seem far removed from those who struggle with mental illness or grief that escapes comfort. The world at large and the private demons that haunt from within may suggest that God has left this sorry mess behind. Far too many of the powers that be in this world, especially the ones that rely on fear and coercion, would just as soon have us stay with that thought. Or, if God is to be admitted at all, then it is a God relegated to a distant future whose only concern is heaven's upkeep.

God is the God of the future, and that is good news to our longing for something better to come. But the truly radical good news resides in the fact that God is not content to rest up until kingdom come. "I am with you" declares, among other things, that matters dear to God's heart like justice and love, compassion and righteousness, are God's pressing desires for the current day. God's presence affirms that we have not been left behind or abandoned to fend for ourselves. Divine presence provides notice of God's transformation of this world for the good. Jesus' life and ministry serves as that notice made incarnate for our sake and for the sake of this God-loved world. As individuals and communities who follow Jesus, God invites us to make those our priorities as we trust holy presence to dispel fear and lead us on the way ahead.

Gracious Favor

What makes the avowal of holy presence a truly gospel gift is the second assertion made in Isaiah and Revelation. God's presence is biased in our favor. "Do not be afraid, for I am *your* God. . . . [God] will dwell with them as *their* God" (AP). We hear the power of those words when we take seriously the settings in which they originally found utterance and audience. "I am *your* God" addresses Jewish exiles in Babylon, captives to imperial power that claimed divine favor proven by force on its side. "I am *your* God" is offered as promise to those who had, for all appearances, fallen into divine disfavor. Had Babylon's might not proved its right to subjugate? Yet Isaiah calls upon the exiles not to fear in the capital city of fear, "for I am *your* God."

Revelation makes the same audacious claim. Stuck in the middle of the sea on a windswept rock far away from the beloved community, John likewise writes that God will dwell with that community as *their* God. When John writes "their," he is not speaking of his imperial captors or the powers they employ to subdue the church by threat and by violence. As the context of the later verses of this passage makes clear, those for whom God is "*their* God" are those who presently mourn and cry, who suffer pain and death.

This favor of God that rests on those in the direst of straits has a long tradition in Judaism and Christianity. The God encountered in Exodus is the God who raised up Hebrew slaves. It is the same God whose favor, according to psalmists and prophets alike, is inclined toward the poor and vulnerable. Such gracious favor continues in the life of Jesus, whose parable of the sheep and the goats ("as you did it to one of the least of these . . .") finds illustration in ministry where Samaritans become role models; little ones are embraced; and room is graciously made for prodigal and elder alike.

The favor of God that banishes fear can be challenging to accept; if God favors us, why does suffering exist in the world? Some might shrug shoulders and say, "God must will it." But that reply risks leaving the impression that God is apathetic toward such sufferings at best and the cause of them at worst. "God wills it" implicitly blames God for sufferings that may in truth be absolutely antithetical to divine purpose. To speak of God's favor requires blending the language of trust with actions of compassion. Often the favor of God awaits conveyance by God's servants.

Part of the challenge to accept the truth of God's favor that banishes fear derives from unhealthy views of self. Some quarters of the church have successfully proclaimed the message of utter depravity ("you are a corrupt sinner to the core"), while remaining silent about the message of original blessing ("you are made in the image of God, part of a creation God deemed good"). As a result, some find the grace and favor of God difficult to accept for their own lives out of a warped sense of self that sees only the bad and cannot imagine the good.

Part of the challenge to accept the favor of God that banishes fear derives from conceit and arrogance that disparages not self but other. The extension of God's favor toward those with whom I agree or whom I resemble is fine. *But clearly God's favor would not extend to the likes of those who . . .* ; let us pause here to consider the names or labels we have heard (or used) to complete that thought. Examples abound.

Since I move largely among liberal folk, at least in my religious circles, let me confess that I am sometimes struck by the way we are tolerant of all but those we deem intolerant. Then, we wax intolerant to rival the best (or worst) of them! Having grown up in St. Louis in the late fifties and early sixties, I also have more than a passing awareness of how such labels have often been framed and phrased based on racial prejudice. In more recent times, when prominent religious leaders comment on public airwaves that 9/11 represented God's punishment on America for abortion or gay rights—well, we keep adding to the list as we go. In the process, the word of God's favor gets obscured by the fog of our pet fears and scapegoats.

The word of God's favor aims to loose us from the fear of those who are strangers to us but who are in truth no strangers to the grace of God. The word of God's favor seeks to lift us up from self-deprecating judgments that leave us emotionally and spiritually crippled. The favor of God invites words and actions of compassion on behalf of those unable to trust and hope. The favor of God endeavors to replace the paralyzing view of God as one who is out to get us (or our enemies) with the saving truth of God as one who advocates for our good and the good of all creation.

Saving Advocacy

Biblical scholars use the term *salvation oracle* for prophetic passages that describe God's promises of deliverance. Isaiah 41 and Revelation 21 are such declarations of God's salvation. But while the word of salvation begins by stating *who* God is ("with us," "for us"), God's saving necessarily moves on to *what* God *does*. In those actions we come to see God's salvation in acts of advocacy. So what does God promise to do that "saves"? Revelation speaks of the result of those actions: death will be no more; mourning, crying, and pain will be no more. The Isaiah passage singles out three actions of God's saving activity: strengthen, help, uphold.

Hebrew has a number of words that express a sense of strength, ranging in meaning from hardness to physical prowess to power. What does Isaiah have in mind when he writes, according to the New Revised Standard Version (emphasis added), [God] "will *strengthen* you"? In Joshua and Deuteronomy, this Hebrew word *amats,* occurs no fewer than seven times in pairings that the NRSV translates as "be strong and bold" (Deut. 31:6, 7, 23) or "be strong and courageous" (Josh. 1:6, 9, 18). So when we read Isaiah's promises of God's saving activity of "strengthening," hear the promise of salvation as this: God will give you courage and boldness.

For those exiles—and for us—that meaning makes perfect sense. The strength God gives is not some supernatural manipulation of physical strength so we can beat up the bad guys on their terms and give *them* something to be afraid about. That was the usual moral of the story of those old Westerns with which this chapter began. And that, far too many times, has been the fallback position of those in power, whether religious or political, as a way to deal with those with whom we are in conflict. We outmuscle them. In contrast, God's saving work in Isaiah 41:10 involves infusing us with courage. God's saving act emboldens exiles, exactly the gift needed so that truth can be told—the truth of God's presence and favor that breaks the hold of fear.

Our liturgies of confession form one practice of such truth-telling. To fears and sin that hold us back and weigh us down, we say: "No more. You are not the future. The future is God—and God has promised the gift of forgiveness." We are emboldened to face what we have done with the grace of what God has done and promises to do. Those confessions provide rehearsals for more public confessions of those truths by individuals and communities of faith. God would also embolden us to speak such truth with courage to those who would play on our fears and rely on our silenced timidity and say—"No more. You are not the future. This will not stand. We trust in God's holy presence and gracious favor." And having said that, we then live that truth.

But God's actions go beyond encouraging and emboldening. Listen to the next promise of God proclaimed by Isaiah: "I will help you." God is our *helper*. Think about that word for a moment, and in particular how it can be misunderstood. Sometimes we hear the term *helper* as referring to one who is subjugated to another or under his or her authority. Part of the twisting of that term may trace all the way back to Genesis, where the narrative of Eve's creation is prefaced by God's thinking out loud that "I will make him [Adam] a *helper* as his partner" (Gen. 2:18, emphasis added). From those words has flowed a river of misconception about the alleged scriptural subjugation of women because Eve is deemed a "helper." What we conveniently forget are the many passages that use the word *helper* in reference to God. Those passages do not make of God a lackey or a subordinate. They make God a help in times of need, which is precisely the message of Isaiah. So when we follow the lead of boldness in declaring faith and resisting fear, we do so with the promise of God as helper in those times and places where faith confronts the powers of fear.

From strengthening and helping comes God's promised saving act of "upholding" in Isaiah 41. When have you experienced being held up by another—emotionally, physically, spiritually, all of the above? Years ago, a youth leader and I decided to swim across a mountain lake as a shortcut back to the youth group camp. Halfway across, the cold water succeeded in sapping my strength. Arms and legs stopped working; I called out for help. Harvey took hold of me and swam me safely to shore. When I think of what *uphold* means, my mind and body float back to that experience. And there have been many others like it, where I have been emotionally and spiritually held up. Saved. What about you?

I am not blind to the truth that such deliverance does not always come as we would have wanted, when we wanted, to whom we wanted. God's promise of upholding does not wave a hand of denial over all the sinking we see around us—and sometimes feel within us. In ways that move into mystery, God's upholding may take more than a lifetime to find final assurance of. To say otherwise risks callousness in the face of a suffering world. But *not* to affirm the upholding of God we have experienced and that we ultimately entrust ourselves and our destiny to, would neglect what God promises to do so that we do not perish in fear—but live toward hope.

God's Presence, Favor, and Advocacy—and Not Living Afraid

We are not alone in this world. God is with us. We do not live in isolation. We do not need to live afraid. God is with us, not as a vengeful tyrant or a disinterested clockmaker who wound up this intricate universe only to sit back and watch it run its course. The God who is *with* us is the God who is *for* us. God harbors a bias in favor of an entire creation deemed good by God's own word, in favor of human life fashioned in the divine image. God's favor runs so deep and comes with such commitment that God made such favor incarnate (John 1:14). We do not need to live afraid.

God's advocacy consists of God's saving actions: past, present, and promised. Such advocacy takes form when God bestows courage and boldness on us to speak and live by the faith we claim and in which we are claimed by holy presence and gracious favor. Such advocacy takes shape when God helps those whose need for aid surpasses our capabilities. Contrary to one popular opinion, God does help those who cannot help themselves. Such advocacy takes hold as God upholds us when and where we might otherwise flounder and give in to fear. God's presence and favor, whether mediated through Spirit or sacrament, community or scripture, neighbor or stranger, acts to save us. We need not live afraid.

So if God acts to save us from living afraid, what are the markers of life loosed from fear? Each of the remaining five chapters explores a single movement of faith made possible by God's saving actions and accompanying declarations of "do not fear." For the first and most foundational of those movements, the next chapter turns to Abraham and Mary. "Do not be afraid," God says to them—and to us—for the sake of exercising trust.

SPIRITUAL EXERCISE #1

Recall an experience that brought home to you the realization that God *is* with us—with you. Do you remember any fear that may have been in the background of that experience:

- a struggle with discerning God,
- a question about God raised by an experience of yours or someone close to you?

How did the recognition of holy presence—God with us, God with you—unfold?

In what ways do you sense holy presence in this moment around you and within you now?

Observe a time of relaxed, unrushed, unfearful prayer centered on the gift of God's presence.

SPIRITUAL EXERCISE #2

Imagine a voice speaking your name aloud and then saying: "I am your God." Repeat those words aloud four times using the following pattern:

- Each time emphasize a different word (*I, am, your, God*).
- Pause and reflect after each of those times:

  —At this time and place in your life, what might God be saying to you?

  —To which of your fears do these words speak?

Prayerfully reflect on the gift and challenge of accepting the word and scope of God's favor.

SPIRITUAL EXERCISE #3

Consider the verbs of Isaiah's three promises of God's saving actions: strengthen, help, uphold. Choose one of these three that best recalls a particular experience of God's acting in your life.

Record a journal entry or create a piece of art or craftwork that reflects on the following:

- In what ways or through what persons did God strengthen, help, or uphold you?
- What fears were part of your life at the time of this experience?
- What do you carry from this experience that might help you now not to live afraid?
- Who might this experience prepare you to strengthen, help, or uphold today?

SPIRITUAL EXERCISE #4

The promises of Isaiah and the vision of Revelation invite us to meditate upon what it means to stand, rest, trust, or act in the awareness of God's presence.

- Where and when do you best experience the gift of holy presence?
- What does such presence bring to your life and spirit?
- What does such presence call forth from you?

Light a candle, or do some other act, that makes you mindful of being in God's presence *now*.

Relish the thought of being in holy presence. Place whatever fears you may be aware of into that presence. And having given over those fears, give thanks to God.

PART II

do not live afraid...

3

For the Sake of Trust

GENESIS 15:1-6
LUKE 1:26-38

———

THE LATE CHILD PSYCHOLOGIST Erik Erikson originated a theory of childhood development that still finds wide acceptance today. He maintained that children face eight stages of development. Erikson further saw the successful attainment of those stages to be dependent upon maturation in the stage(s) previous to it. He alleged that the first of those stages, and thus the foundation for the rest, is learned (or not) in the first year or so of life: trust. A failure to learn trust, while not ruling out development in later years, creates a major complicating factor for the child all along the way. Trust forms the bedrock upon which all other growth relies.

Trust involves making oneself open, some might say vulnerable, to another. Fear, on the other hand, is all about closing oneself off. Fear may mimic trust in the way that someone who is constantly bullied by another might place himself or herself at that other's mercy in hope of shielding themselves from the abuse. But in such a relationship, fear will always hold the upper hand. For what if that mercy is withdrawn? Fear thrives on threat. In contrast, trust thrives on openness to another in relationship. Trust relies on the assurance, born of experience or accepted testimony, that the other seeks your good. Trust cannot be coerced and still be trust. Trust can only be invited in hope of its free acceptance.

Consider the parallels to Erikson's stages of development in the spiritual journey. Before faith takes shape as a body of organized beliefs reflected in formal creeds or statements, faith is at its heart trust in God. Faith opens life, values, and destiny to the purposes of God. Trust in God is not throwing ourselves on the mercy of an otherwise ill-disposed God in order to avoid retribution. Trust in God grows out of the conviction that God seeks our good. God's promises disclose that gracious disposition. Faith becomes our determination that God and those promises are trustworthy. We need not live afraid because of God's trustworthiness and the goodness of God's purposes.

God approaches both Abram and Mary in this chapter's scripture passages with the identical declaration: "Do not be afraid." Why? What is at stake in these relationships cannot be grounded in fear's threat or coercion. The promises that await both characters will rely on the practice of trust by an over-the-hill patriarch and a teenaged madonna. As in Erikson's theory, everything that will or will not develop in their relationship with God will be based on their openness to leave fear behind for the sake of exercising trust. What is true for Abram and Mary is true for us as well. Everything that will or will not develop in *our* relationship with God will be based on *our* openness to leave fear behind for the sake of exercising trust.

Human Trust and God's Initiative

Notice where these passages about Abram and Mary begin. Abram receives a vision. Mary gets an angel's visit. Right off the bat, that may send up red flags for some. *Well, I'd be a person of faith too if God showed up in a dream or an angel dropped by on my doorstep.* I admit, there are days and nights when I'd like to have such a definitive experience of divine intervention to hang my faith's hat upon. But what if these details of God's abrupt entry into their lives have less to do with Abram and Mary—and even us—and more to do with God? What do these openings with holy visions and visits reveal about God?

I would say trust and faith begin as a gift extended by God, in the initiative God takes toward us. Let those words sink in a bit. We understand grace as a gift of God. But in Genesis 15 and Luke 1, faith also originates in the unsolicited gift of God's intervention in the lives of these two individuals so that they may exercise trust. Trust begins with God reaching in our direction—not to coerce but to promise.

So where might our faith begin if we take these stories of God's initiative with Abram and Mary as addressing our faith's origins as well? The possibilities are as varied as the experiences and persons who formed the pathways for our being opened to God in trust. We might point to this experience as a youth or to that turning point as an adult. We might recall a friend who guided us or a pastor who challenged us. We might envision a particular church building or an exquisite natural setting that played a significant role in our spiritual growth and development. But here is the common ground, at least as I understand why these narratives of Genesis and Luke open as they do. In every one of those persons, in every one of those places, in every one of those experiences: God was taking the initiative to create and nurture the gift of faith in us, in preparation for when we could make faith our own.

This grounding of faith, not just grace, in the gifting of our lives by God plays a key role in our relationship with God. It serves as a buffer against confusing our exercise of faith with the religious equivalent of pulling ourselves up by the bootstraps. Faith is not a spiritually acceptable form of works-righteousness whereby we earn heavenly merit badges by the degree to which we conjure up faith on our own effort. Trust and faith have their origins in all the ways and all the persons who have been the instruments by which God has gifted us with faith.

So in one sense, any regret we might have about not having visions of God or heavenly visitors is misleading. The letter to the

Hebrews cautions about not neglecting to show hospitality to strangers, for by such hospitality "some have entertained angels without knowing it" (Heb. 13:2). Perhaps we need to look back (and look around) at those who have and who continue to bring to us the gift of faith—and acknowledge that angels have and still do visit us. God takes the initiative with us through some very human instruments, so that we can open ourselves to trust God's promises rather than close ourselves off in fear.

God speaks the word of "do not be afraid" to Abram and Mary. God takes the initiative to free them from fear to exercise trust in God. But after God takes that initiative to encourage their trust, God awaits their response. God does not coerce the answer of trust from their mouths or their wills. Fear uses coercion. Love offers invitation, here in the form of promises, and then waits for trust to be freely chosen.

If we think such freedom is mere window decoration in these stories and in our lives, we misunderstand the character of God who allows us to choose. And if we think that the trust of Abram and Mary proceeds automatically, given the dramatic nature of God's initiatives with them, or if we think trust means our shutting up and stifling questions and exercising blind obedience, we misread these stories and their lessons of faith for our lives. The responses forthcoming from Abram and Mary after hearing "do not be afraid" make clear that the evoking of such trust merits the question of trustworthiness. After all, to set aside fear, they need to know—*we* need to know—whether God can be trusted to see these promises through.

Can God Be Trusted?

The Reverend Billy Graham, in a sermon titled "Faith," told the following story.

I heard of an incident that took place at Niagara Falls. A crowd watched as a man rolled a wheelbarrow filled with two hundred pounds of dirt back and forth on a tight rope across the falls. When he asked, "How many of you believe I can roll a man across?" one spectator very excitedly shouted, "I know you can do it!" He said, "All right, brother, you're first." You couldn't see that man for dust![2]

Now I wouldn't want to bet the family farm on whether that story is factual or not. But I am convinced the story's truth resides in the fact that trust entails risk of self to another. Sometimes the church has done a disservice by trying to domesticate if not eliminate the risk. We cushion hard pews and harder words. We give a wink and a nod when we come to passages about carrying crosses. We water down faith into the formula of what we believe about God rather than staying with faith as the dynamic relationship *with* God. But every now and then, something happens that brings us into the position of that fellow in the story who suddenly sees that trust in God only happens inside the wheelbarrow. Will we flee, or will we get in? Or will we, as Abram and Mary do, seek first to find out if they can trust this wheelbarrow and its owner?

The questions and challenges Abram poses in Genesis 15:2-3 are remarkable when you consider to whom he speaks. "What will you give me?" is Abram's opening volley to God. Abram then immediately inserts an answer born out of his own experience to date, "You have given me no offspring"—which is close to saying, "You have given me *nothing*."

Before we too eagerly charge Abram with ingratitude and disrespect, let us remember that this story line is intimately connected to a time line. When Abram and Sarai followed God's call and left Haran for a land known only as promise, Abram was seventy-five years old and Sarai sixty-five. Sarai was barren. Then the journey began. First to Canaan, then to Egypt. Then they returned north to the Negeb (the desert region separating modern-day Israel and Egypt), and back into Canaan in the southern village of Hebron. And still no child, no heir. And without an heir, all the promised land in the world will do no good, for there will be no one to carry the gift into the next generation and beyond. So Abram's lament that God has given him nothing is technically correct. Abram trusted God by leaving Haran behind. Can God still be trusted?

Mary's reticence to embrace the angel's presence immediately and her words take a more subtle route than Abram. At first Luke notes that the angel's greeting is met by Mary with perplexity, a Greek word that more literally means "to be thoroughly troubled." It shares the same root with the word used to describe Jesus being troubled by his impending betrayal (John 13:21) and the "hour" of crucifixion (John 12:27). So let us not discount the depth of trouble and perplexity Mary experiences. Even after hearing the angel describe the promises for this child she will bear, Mary goes on to pose the telling question: "How can this be?"

Why dwell on the resistance of Abram and Mary to fall lockstep instantaneously, unquestioning, into trust? Their examples ring true to life. Blind trust, unthinking trust, unquestioning trust: God neither finds nor seems to want these from Abram and Mary. Otherwise, God would send them and their questions packing. But God does not do that with them or with us. Trust cannot be coerced. God does not bully Abram and Mary into trusting acceptance for fear of divine disfavor. God reveals that neither they nor we need fear in holy presence. God is not after our fear. God desires our trust. And when questions are raised and, in Abram's case, lament is offered ("what will you give me, for I continue childless") that signals a desire to know if God can be trusted, God responds not with "shush" but with a word and a sign.

For Abram, the word affirms an heir will come. For Mary, the word affirms Spirit will come. But interestingly enough, neither of those words "proves" anything, any more than the signs that God offers. The sign for Abram is a look at the stars: "so shall your descendants be." The sign for Mary is the pregnancy of a once-barren but now pregnant relative. Does the countless number of stars in the firmament *prove* anything about God's trustworthiness? Does the unborn child of Elizabeth *prove* the identity and mission of Mary's promised child? At this point, faith as an act of human will and decision comes into play. God has taken the initiative in seeking these two. God has listened to their wonderings as to whether God really can be trusted. God has answered with further words and signs intended to help convey the scope and nature of what has been promised. But now the focus shifts from God to Abram and Mary. Both will have to decide for themselves the truth of the assertion that concludes the angel's words to Mary: "Nothing will be impossible with God."

Is that true—not just in the abstract but in Abram's continued patience for an heir and in Mary's receptivity to unexpected motherhood? Is nothing impossible, which is to say, can God be trusted to make possibilities where barrenness and scandal would otherwise hold the upper hand? Abram and Mary had to decide, had to *trust*, for themselves. Just so, you and I have to decide, have to *trust*, for ourselves. That is the nature of faith's gift and its call. And we now turn to the meaning of that decision to entrust ourselves to the God of extraordinary possibilities.

Possibility Trusting

Try this. Go online and do a search on "possibility thinking." The number of hits are overwhelming. You will find sites for motivational speakers, offers of books or tapes on the subject, even one on golf possibility thinking if that is your interest. In the religious world, Robert Schuller is perhaps the best-known expositor and marketer of possibility thinking.

Possibility thinking has much to offer. Dwelling on negatives can indeed be a shortcut to dragging down attitude and expectations. I would add only this caveat. Thinking, whether possibility-wise or otherwise, can take you only so far. What you *think* about someone or God can be interesting. But where does it lead? A seminary professor taught me a litmus test for all theological assertions and confessions: *so what?* The most eloquent of statements, if it remains only in the realm of abstract thought, gets us nowhere. If possibility thinking, while well and good, does not affect the conduct of our lives and relationships, it is empty.

That is why I titled this section "Possibility *Trusting*." Genesis and Luke do not narrate the stories of Abram and Mary because these two *think* good thoughts about God. They remember and celebrate their stories because Abram and Mary open themselves, risk themselves, in trust to God. Genesis offers a bare-bones sketch of this movement when it says Abram "believed the LORD." Luke's record of Mary's response is more descriptive: "Here am I, the servant of the Lord; let it be with me according to your word."

"Let it be."

Some may hear Mary's reply and recall the Beatles' song that takes its title from her words. Some may hear "let it be" as a synonym for "leave it alone." This much the Beatles have right: "let it be" is a word of wisdom. This much the "leave it alone" hearing has right: "let it be" invites a letting go of something. And the wisdom of what must be let go is fear.

For Mary, it is the fear of being asked to be part of something that has no precedent in creation, much less in her life. It is the fear of wondering *why me?* It is the fear of not knowing the "end game" in terms of what all of this will mean for her and her child down the road. When Simeon later prophesies to Mary that her child is "destined for the falling and the rising of many" and "a sword will pierce your own soul" (Luke 2:34, 35), such fears seem well founded. This is the risk that comes with entrusting oneself to God or another. The causes for fear are not automatically dissipated, rendered harmless, or cast out of the picture. In Mary's case, her response of "let it be" signifies a willing trust in God and an openness to receive the future, whatever it brings. She trusts in holy possibilities for good. "Let it be."

Do we practice the discipline of "possibility trusting"? That is, do we risk opening ourselves to trust holy possibilities for our lives? The question is not rhetorical. We ought not assume Mary and Abram were the last ones God sought for such trust. Such trust opens us to look beyond the ordinary limits that hold us back and to make the leap of "let it be" where others can only catalogue reasons for fear or failure. The leap of trust may lead us in the direction of relationships with or advocacy on behalf of others who are our communities' versions of "untouchables." Did not Jesus go out on a limb speaking to a Samaritan woman? The leap of trust may lead us to action that is not met with universal acclaim. Did not Jesus upset the Temple establishment with some rather untoward turning of tables to make a point? Or perhaps the holy possibilities for our lives come on far more personal terms. Do we yearn for an as yet unidentified newness in our walk with God? Do we sense that if only we could let go of some fear of failure or censure, we could move out of our spiritual rut? If so, let mother Mary whisper her words of wisdom to you: "Let it be."

Trust and Not Living Afraid

In an earlier book in which I considered the Annunciation story, I wrote this about Mary: "It is one thing to affirm that God is free to do as God wills in this world. The real crunch comes in allowing God the freedom and trust to act in one's own life."[3] Mary and Abram make that leap. They set aside the fear that might hold them back from entrusting themselves to God.

If nature indeed abhors a vacuum, then to let go of fear and not live afraid requires something to take fear's place in our hearts, minds, and wills. The stories of Mary and Abram reveal that "something" to be trust. What do our stories, our lives, reveal? We do not create such trust all by ourselves. The stories of Abram and Mary remind us of God's initiative in creating cause for us to trust. A rereading of our stories and lives may reveal similar initiatives through those who have played a role in shaping our faith and leading us into relationship with God and Christ's community. Some of us may even have had mystical experiences that gifted us with faith. Whether in a vision that came in a dream or in a friend who accompanied us on the path that led to holy encounter, God continues to bestow and encourage the gift of faith.

And having gifted and encouraged our trust, God patiently and graciously awaits its exercise by us. Will we trust God? Will we open ourselves to holy purposes and possibilities? Will we set fear aside, as God invites us to, and place in its stead trust in God? The freedom to say and to live "let it be" is ours by the grace of God.

Where we go and what we do with that trust opens us to the next chapter's theme: do not live afraid for the sake of vocation.

SPIRITUAL EXERCISE #1

Recall several persons who strongly influenced your journey with God. In what ways might their impact on you be related to God's taking the initiative to gift your life with the possibility of (deeper) trust? Offer a prayer of thanks for each of those individuals.

Consider someone with whom you live, work, or share community, for whom trust is hard at this moment. How might God work through you to gift his or her life with the possibility of trust?

SPIRITUAL EXERCISE #2

Look back on an exercise of trust that did not come easily to you.

- What formed the hurdles or obstacles?
- How did those obstacles relate to the "trustworthiness" of the one to be trusted (or not)?
- What made your trust possible; what would have made it impossible?

Consider an aspect of your present faith journey where faith does not come easily for you. Be in earnest and honest prayer to God about it: your hopes, your questions, your fears. Keep an open mind and heart to what and where God may be leading you.

SPIRITUAL EXERCISE #3

"Let it be." What has it taken in the past for you to reach the point where you offered such words to God? If you have never reached that point, consider why that has been true. In either case, consider whether it might be a word and prayer fit for this moment.

- What might trust in God encourage you to accept or take on at this moment?
- What fears might trust in God encourage you to let go of?
  Pray for God's grace and strength to let it be . . . and to let it go.

Spiritual Exercise #4

Call to mind the times when your trust in God has been most important and most clear to you. What made them so?

Imagine someone who felt he or she had no cause to consider God worthy of trust.

- What could you tell him or her from your life experience?
- What could you show him or her of God by your trustworthiness toward him or her?

Offer a prayer of thanks for the ways God has shown that your trust was well-placed.

Pray for even deeper trust in God—and for opportunities to help others come to such trust.

4

For the Sake of Vocation

DEUTERONOMY 31:7-8
LUKE 5:1-11

———

IN 1933 THE UNITED STATES was deep into what has been deemed the Great Depression. Sparked by the stock market crash of 1929, it plunged the nation into a financial crisis that spiraled out of control. It cost Herbert Hoover a second term as president. When his successor was inaugurated as the next president in March of 1933, Franklin Roosevelt faced the daunting task of pushing a legislative agenda to address the effects of the Depression. Perhaps more importantly, he faced the challenge of instilling public confidence that the economy and society itself could be restored. So what did Roosevelt affirm at the outset of his first inaugural address to broach that possibility? "The only thing we have to fear is fear itself." He went on to identify this fear to be feared as whatever could paralyze "needed efforts to convert retreat into advance." To engage the work of recovery, people had to set fear aside.

The need to banish fear for the sake of vocation, national or individual, is not unique to the era of the New Deal. All manner of work can be paralyzed by fear. Sometimes the fear relates to consequences for the considered action. You witness an accident where someone has been hurt. Do you stop and render aid, or do you shy away for fear of becoming involved? Sometimes the fear relates to implications for the proposed action. Jonah fled God's call to go to Nineveh. The end of Jonah's story revealed that his fear was not what the Ninevites might do but what God might do. "'That is why I fled to Tarshish at the beginning; for I knew that you are a gracious God'" (Jon. 4:2).

Setting fear aside for the sake of vocation is this chapter's focus. Narratives about Joshua and Peter illumine the way. Both were told not to fear or be afraid for the sake of work soon to be entrusted into their care. In the case of Joshua, that work took up the baton passed on by another. In the case of Peter, that work initially would come by following the lead of another. In either case, fear could have held them back. Whether it would or not depended on their decision to trust the promissory word of "do not fear"—and then to live and work accordingly. Whether fear holds us back or not depends on the same decision of trust in the promise of "do not fear," whose answer comes in the vocations we then exercise or flee.

Vocation as "Called Out"

The word *vocation* used in this chapter's title may need some unpacking. In my youth, vocational schools were alternative secondary schools that trained young men and women for trades. Vocation was literally understood as a job, quite often some form of manual labor. In some religious traditions, vocation was and remains closely connected with ordained or some other form of "set apart" ministry. An Internet search on "vocation" will show how closely we still associate the word with the discerning or practice of an intentional religious career path.

So what does this chapter have in mind when speaking of vocation—particularly of not living afraid for the sake of exercising vocation? Contrary to the first example (vocational school), vocation is not limited to job. Contrary to the second example (religious vocation), vocation is not exclusive to the domain of intentional religious careers. Vocation in this chapter goes back to the word's very derivation: "voiced, called." The resemblance of vocation to "vocal" is no coincidence. Those who hear the word of God or Christ addressing them are those who are called. Those who hear the word of God or Christ saying "do not fear" are those called to live free from the domination of fear. So based on such callings, what is our vocation?

Some years back, my denomination provided the following quote in its annual financial-appeal resources: "Stewardship is everything you do after you say, 'I believe.'" I agree with that. But since our associations with stewardship are sometimes overly concerned with budgets, pie charts, and pledge forms, let me offer this paraphrase to identify the common ground of our vocation. Vocation is everything you do after you say, "I trust God."

Vocation involves work, make no mistake about that. But work and career are not synonymous. Nor does one have to enter a formal religious career path, as professional or volunteer, to have a vocation. The call of God upon our lives bestows vocation. How and whether we respond to that call forms our embrace or avoidance of vocation. The narratives of Joshua and Peter relate stories of being called out and given a vocation. Deuteronomy describes Moses as "summoning" Joshua. The Hebrew verb *qara* there literally means "to call" or "to name." Joshua has been named, called out of the congregation of Israel for a purpose, a *vocation*. "'You are the one who will go with this people into the land.'"

"You are the one." As you listen to the words spoken by God through Moses to Joshua, can you hear in them any soundings of your own name being spoken, when you have been "called out" for the sake of some vocation entrusted to your care and action? Perhaps you have associated such a calling and vocation with the context of marital life. When you heard the officiant speak your name and ask if you would promise to love the individual standing beside you, that was an entrusting of vocation to you: the vocation to love. Or maybe you have heard your name singled out in some other setting, whether spoken aloud or heard from within, where you knew you were the one being called to a task. That was vocation. Perhaps we in the church do not spend enough time helping others or ourselves to hear or speak the word that evokes the sense and stirring of vocation. Perhaps we have spent too much time focusing on vocation to formal religious careers for the sake of buoying up depleting ranks of ministerial candidates and neglected the nurture of vocation we all share as servants of Christ.

If Joshua's vocation arises out of a clear and direct call issued to him, Peter's vocation comes more subtly, at least at first. Initially Jesus only asks for the use of Peter's boat as a speaking platform. Perhaps a fishless night readied Peter for a little distraction from the routine. Only later does Jesus speak more pointedly, and he does so in reference and even in slight contradiction of what Peter considered his vocation to be. Jesus tells Peter to set out for deep water and to let down nets usually employed only at night, not what an experienced fisherman would do. But the weight of the catch and the weight of the situation eventually catch up with Peter, setting the stage for his being called to a new vocation.

It takes a while sometimes for us to catch on to the calls that bring vocation. Maybe we thought we would join the church for the sake of the kids, to give them a good upbringing. Or maybe we felt something was missing in our lives, something that others talked about; and we went on a spiritual fishing trip to see what might come our way. But then, over time or in a flash, it dawns on us. There is more to this than what's in it for the kids or to pique our curiosity. This searching for what might come *to* us has become an urging to consider what might be called to come *from* us. In those times we hear our names spoken in tandem with what our trust in God might be calling us to do.

Then and there we find ourselves called to vocation. But then and there we also have to face the question What will we do?

"Go Away from Me!"

One of the things that makes the biblical witness so compelling to me is its willingness to portray its "heroes" in all-too-human colors. We have touched on the story of Jonah. When God called him to head east for Nineveh, Jonah hightailed it to the first westbound ship he could find. When God called Moses and presented him with the vocation of leading Israel out of the house of bondage, Moses claimed to be "slow of speech and slow of tongue." When all else failed, Moses cut to the chase with God: "Please send someone else" (Exod. 4:13).

Lest we too easily criticize Moses for his reluctance and resistance, let us keep in mind not only what is being asked of him in terms of vocation—but who is doing the asking. Being called out by God for some task is no trivial matter—not for Moses and not for us. Consider what is claimed in God's calling of us. We are named, singled out, by the Holy One who spun the stars into being and set the tides into motion. We are named, called out by the Holy One so full of love for this creation as to take on the vulnerability of human existence to show the extent of that love. Those would be humbling thoughts to most folks. Are they to you? No wonder Moses later charged Joshua to be "bold." It would have taken no small degree of boldness to accept that God was singling out Joshua to be the one to succeed Moses in leading Israel. Then again, it would take no small degree of boldness to contemplate God's singling you out with that same word of "you are the one." Yet that is precisely the meaning of vocation, of our being called by God. Boldness does not come in an arrogant brashness that would congratulate God on making such a wise choice as me. Rather, boldness comes in openness to the call of the Holy One, who affixes my name to holy purposes. Such boldness does not come easily, even for the brash among us, when fear looms large.

Consider Peter, the disciple with whom we normally associate boldness. When Peter realized, however imperfectly or tentatively, the nature of the one whose baffling command had put his and his partners' boat in jeopardy of sinking, he pleaded for Jesus to go away. Peter attributed that plea to his being a sinful man in the presence of one who had brought about this remarkable catch. But on another level, Peter's "go away from me" might also be heard as a subtle desire to keep Jesus at arm's length. Why? If Jesus can do this, what else might he do—and perhaps even more to the point, what else might Jesus ask Peter to do?

"Go away from me, Lord, for I am a sinful man [or woman]!" Peter in that boat is not all that different from Moses before the bush or Jonah before his place of call . . . or you and me. We can always summon reasons (we would not call them excuses, would we?) for why we are not the right persons for this job or that task: "Someone else would be better at that. Come on, God, I'm a sinner." Or, in place of "sinner," we might insert whatever else we think might get us off the hook, allowing us to fade back into the unnamed crowd of the uninvolved and unengaged. But something is at work there in offering those rationales and backpedalings, and that something is fear. Look carefully at how Jesus responds to Peter. Jesus neither agrees nor disagrees with Peter's assessment of his sinfulness. Jesus doesn't even acknowledge it. Instead, the first words out of Jesus' mouth are, "Do not be afraid." What Jesus hears in Peter's words are fear—and nothing else will be righted, including vocation, until fear is removed.

How do we express our fear of vocation? Do we retreat like Moses or Peter into what is wrong with us? Do we shield ourselves with prideful arrogance, where openness to vocation is blocked by the determination that "I am the one who makes the calls around here!" Examples of both sides of this fear-driven coin can be found in spiritual journey. Some people do not open themselves to vocation for fear of having no gifts to offer. The church has not always been adept at helping members distinguish between humility and humiliation in spirit. That can result in folks who feel they have nothing to offer shy away from involvements for fear of having that deadening assessment reinforced. Equally detrimental are those who insist vocation, whether their own or others or even that of the church, must always be on their terms. We have likely all suffered a board member—or a pastor—who falls into this latter category. If the truth be told, at one time or another, we may even have been that board member or pastor. Fear drives them and us when we resist anything that calls us out of our comfort zones or suggests we are not the ones in control around here.

But God will not leave us in our fears, whether of our own inadequacies or the presumed inadequacies of others. Whether the fear be having our own weaknesses exposed or our latent but untapped gifts disclosed; whether the fear be losing our control over others or being tapped to assume responsibilities we would prefer to avoid, God declares: "Do not be afraid." Do not let those fears deter you from vocation. Fears are about living in the past. Vocation is about—well, recall Jesus' counsel to Peter who knelt before him in the boat. The first word Jesus speaks to Peter's fearful confession is, "Do not be afraid." But it is not the last word.

"From Now On . . ."

"'From now on you will be catching people'" (Luke 5:10). The first three words in that previous sentence are the key ones when it comes to vocation and not living afraid. They declare that there is a life after setting aside fear; that life is called vocation. For Peter, it was catching people. The "from now on" for Joshua involved bringing Israel into the land. And the "from now on" for us? Vocation is everything we do after we say we trust God.

"From now on." Imagine briefly if your congregation took seriously God's liberating gift of "do not be afraid." Without fear to block or deter vocation, how would you imagine Jesus ending that next sentence: "from now on you will be . . ." What if your congregation no longer feared the things that presently catch ideas in midair and say, "That's well and good, but if we do that, we are liable to—" Or, "I remember when Old First tried that. It cost them members and money." Or, "We can't do that. We've never done that!" Fear can take many forms: fear of rejection, fear of conflict, fear of change—and for some of the avant-garde among us, the fear of the status quo and tradition. When fear runs the program, no matter what its direction, community suffers. But again, imagine fear's disarming in this call to vocation of "from now on." "From now on" is a word that breaks open the future. "From now on" makes possible new starts and not for congregations alone.

Imagine also your setting aside the fears that typically get in your way. What if you took "do not be afraid" to heart? How would your life, how would your involvements, fill in Jesus' words of "from now on you will . . ."? Vocation is all about the "from now on" of our lives. Vocation is about being free and responsible to love God and serve others from this moment forward in our lives and to do so without fear.

The truth of that, at least in the biblical witness, comes in the fact that "do not be afraid" is not said once and for all so that fear never makes another appearance. Fear keeps coming back. Even for the biblical "celebrities," vocation gets tried again and again by fear's return. This will not be the last time Peter confronts fear, with a less-than-stellar immediate outcome for his vocation. Had Peter not feared when Jesus taught of a Messiah who would suffer, Peter would not have taken Jesus aside and rebuked him. Had Peter not feared around the fire in the high priest's courtyard, Peter would not have denied Jesus.

"Do not be afraid," just like "you are forgiven," are needed companions throughout our lives. We strive to be faithful followers, to be strong and bold in vocation. But sometimes, strength wavers. Sometimes, boldness weakens or mutates into arrogance. By and large, those experiences come because of fear. "Do not be afraid" can fade into the background all too quickly when tragedy or injustice or downright ignorance holds sway.

But God does not give up on us. God does not strip us of our calling in those times when we realize that even having nothing to fear but fear itself still leaves us with a considerable antagonist to face. Rather, God calls us out—out of sin, out of fear—and gives us the possibility of a new day. As with Peter, "from now on" is the word that offers and restores our vocation.

Vocation and Not Living Afraid

Years ago I came across an expression used in an early twentieth-century sermon by Richard Roberts. One phrase stays with me. He declared that the church suffered from "a glut of unutilized grace."[4] His argument ran something like this: We feast ("glut," as in gluttony) on grace's bounties, but we do little with the energy grace provides to engage in similarly gracious activity and service.

Roberts's assessment resonates with the aim of this chapter. Time and again in scripture we are offered the gift of "do not be afraid." We celebrate that gift of freedom from fear; we feast at the banquet table of its assurance, but what then do we do with that freedom and assurance? How do we live our lives without fear, freed by the gospel not only to reorient our attitudes from fearful inclinations but to unleash fear-freed action?

Vocation is all about the lived response we make to the gospel's gift. That is why the title of this book is *Do Not Live Afraid* rather than *Do Not Be Afraid*. Not being afraid is God's gift to us, made accessible by our trust in its assurance. But the gospel does not end with altered states of mind. Otherwise, love could be fulfilled by thinking good thoughts. Good thoughts and intentions are important, but the gospel of Jesus Christ calls us to more. It calls us to vocation. Our God-given vocation is to translate the gospel's gift of not being afraid into the gospel's practice of not living afraid. That vocation belongs to the whole church. You and I are the ones called to its practice in a world dominated by fear, a practice that leads us to provide in word and deed our witness to God.

SPIRITUAL EXERCISE #1

"The only thing we have to fear is fear itself." Recall a time when your life was beset by fear(s).

- In what ways did your fear(s) impact your life; your faith?
- What helped you to move beyond your fear(s)? How does that experience shape your understanding of what the quote above means?

How does your experience shape your hearing of this book's invitation not to live afraid?

Pray for God's presence and assurance to help you move past some fear you face now.

SPIRITUAL EXERCISE #2

Remember an experience when you felt yourself singled out for some task.

- In what ways was it frightening, challenging, encouraging, assuring?
- By whom were you singled out—and how did that influence your reaction to it?

As you think about that experience and as you consider this chapter:

- What do you perceive to be your vocation as a follower of Jesus?
- In what ways did you come to experience and understand that calling?
- Where do you draw strength to practice that vocation with boldness?

Spiritual Exercise #3

Read Peter's words to Jesus after the catch: "Go away from me, Lord, for I am a sinful man!" At what times in your life have you sought to distance yourself from God? What were your reasons and what fears might they have involved?

Imagine yourself as Peter. What is going on inside as you say those words?

Read Psalm 139:1-18. Where do you see connections between the psalmist and Peter, the psalmist and you?

Offer a prayer of thanks to God for grace and vocation that will not let us go.

Spiritual Exercise #4

Where in your life have you been holding on to a fear?

Name that place, that fear, aloud and then say aloud Jesus' words to Peter: "Do not be afraid; from now on you will . . ."

Imagine how Jesus would finish that gift of vocation to you. Freed of that place, freed of that fear, what would God have you do "from now on"?

Pray for God's help and grace in practicing that vocation from now on.

5

For the Sake of Witness

JEREMIAH 1:4-10
MATTHEW 28:8-10

ONCE UPON A TIME in a land far away, I was a Cub Scout. I still have my red-and-gray Pinewood Derby racer. My ability to knot a tie came from one of the assignments in the Cub Scout manual. Much has been forgotten or left behind in various moves over the years. But one of the activities I still recall involved a simple exercise in giving directions. I had to verbally direct someone from my house to the fire hall and the police station. I recall practicing this with my father. First, I had to receive the directions myself, when I wasn't sure about street names or numbers of blocks involved. Then I would rehearse what I learned from him and from my own experience in order to prepare myself to give the directions at the next den meeting.

Looking back, I realized that exercise was a small but important lesson about giving witness. Calling it "witness" might sound odd. Aren't we concerned here with giving voice to our testimony about God? Yes, and that Cub Scout routine imparted an aspect of value that my years of Sunday school did not. In Sunday school the adults (or the curriculum) did most of the talking. Faith was voiced by what they said or what the multiple-choice or fill-in-the-blank curriculum dictated. Except in our memory work recitations before Mrs. Schaefer, we students did not often have extended times to voice the words by which we were being raised.

To be sure, the witness to which faith calls us is far more than a child's giving directions to the fire hall, but that's not a bad place to start. For we might understand witness, in one sense, as "directions" to the whereabouts of God or God's ways in this world. Is witness not our pointing the way, at least the way we have experienced, to holy encounter and faithful living?

As a Cub Scout, my "witness" in giving directions was called for by the manual's learning objectives. But what is at stake, and what fears may arise when our witness is summoned for the sake of testimony about the presence and purposes of God in and for our lives and the world?

Setting fear aside for the sake of such witness is the theme of this chapter. The Bible passages that guide us in this exploration are the calls given to Jeremiah and the women at Jesus' tomb to serve as God's witnesses. Let me offer a word about what distinguishes witness from vocation as explored in the last chapter. Vocation is how we live out our calling in response to God. How we live or what we do may or may not direct someone's attention to God, at least overtly. Witness, on the other hand, intends that our words and actions direct purposeful attention to the God who is their source and motivation. Saint Francis of Assisi is credited with the line: "Preach the gospel at all times, and if necessary, use words." That may comfort those of us who shy away from direct speech about God or have been turned off by verbal bludgeonings some confuse with witness. Yet even as Saint Francis implies, words may be necessary, especially when we need to explicitly link our faith with action. That is the role of witness: to intentionally give voice, our voice, to the ways of God for the sake of opening individuals and communities to transformative encounter with God. It is to such witness and the fears it must face that we now turn through the stories of Jeremiah and the women.

Witness as Triangulation

In the field of communication and relationships, triangulation involves bringing a third party into a relationship between one person or group and another. Intentionally or unintentionally, that third party may become either a conduit for information among the parties or a referee between the original two when conflict arises. Sometimes the neutral third party readily takes on this role out of a desire to be helpful or controlling. Pastors are notorious for taking on or being assigned this role in congregational life. Several problems arise with triangulation. Two individuals (or groups) who should be talking to each other do not, if opting for the third-party filter. Beyond that, the three parties in the triangle often end up shifting roles. The one who came in as mediator is drawn into taking sides, and a complicated situation worsens.

Why speak of witness as triangulation, given these negatives? Recall the role of witness as described earlier: "to intentionally give voice, our voice, to the ways of God for the sake of opening individuals and communities to transformative encounter with God." The parties involved in the transaction that is faith's witness are these: those who offer it ("our voice"), those to whom it is directed ("individuals and communities"), and God. It is a triangle. The witness intercedes or is inserted between the audience and God. To speak of a witness as one "inserted between" grows out of the Jeremiah passage. The role of God's witness or prophet there is not so much chosen as reluctantly accepted. Jeremiah did not seek out God. God appointed Jeremiah—or, in modern communication theory, Jeremiah got triangulated between God and Israel.

That may sound harsh to modern ears, nurtured in the language of choice about the free agency of human beings to exercise their will. But the book of Jeremiah, one of the most evocative of an individual prophet's emotions and struggles, is not a personal spiritual journal. This book's witness centers on God's sovereign purposes. Those purposes will hold sway in spite of kings who seem to have power but do not, in spite of traditions that would seem to last forever but do not, in spite of hopes that seem dashed but are not, despite prophets reluctant to accept such a call.

God's sovereign purposes that will not fail or ultimately be deterred form the backbone of faith's witness for Jeremiah and for us. That strengthens our witness but also evokes humility on our part. Our witness is not grounded in how persuasively we can gain others' agreement or how cleverly we shape words that others find appealing or how strongly we enforce our will so that others do what we intend. We are triangulated in witness—that is, the word we bring and the purposes we acknowledge flow from God. They point both back and forward to God. Our witness's aim is not to make devotees of our personal opinions *about* God but to open others to the transforming presence and power *of* God.

For Jeremiah, those others are the *nations*, a Hebrew word also translated as "Gentiles." For the women, those others are the *brothers*, followers dispersed by crucifixion now in need of gathering and sending by resurrection. These stories depict God's triangulating Jeremiah and the women so that they serve as witnesses between God and outsiders and insiders alike. But what of us? Who might be the ones outside or inside our circles to whom God would send us as witnesses? What fears might hold us back, fears addressed by God's word of "do not be afraid"?

Finding Our Voice by Facing Our Fears

"We've a Story to Tell to the Nations." "How Can I Keep from Singing?" "I Love to Tell the Story." "Ask Ye What Great Thing I Know." "Go, Tell It on the Mountain." "Pass It On." "Here I Am, Lord." We come from a faith tradition that is rich in hymns and songs that celebrate our witness. We lift our voices to sing these affirmations in corporate worship, often with great energy and strong harmonies. But how at ease and energetic are we at lifting our voices in witness outside the safety of sanctuaried worship?

Witness risks becoming monotone when it is reduced to what we pay the preacher to do for us. Does energy flee from our throats when we find ourselves in a situation where a word about God's transforming presence and power will have to come, if it comes at all, from us? The books of Jeremiah and Matthew report "do not be afraid" as spoken to Jeremiah and the women in preparation for their calls to witness. What fears might they have had in need of assuaging—not as a point of historical curiosity but as insight into the fears that may block our witness?

The assurance to Jeremiah contains a revealing insight into one of those fears: "'do not be afraid *of them*'" (emphasis added). Who are they? In the context of the previous verse, they are "all to whom I send you." The opening verse in that passage notes Jeremiah is appointed as prophet to the *nations*, a term that usually references populations outside of Israel, geographically and theologically. But as the book of Jeremiah unfolds, those with whom Jeremiah comes into greatest conflict and perhaps has greatest reason to fear are those within his own country, as well as his own family (9:4).

The fear of others, whether strangers or members of our own circles, can stifle our voice and witness. With strangers, the fear leans toward the unknown. We may not know how they will react to our words, and so we remain silent. With friends and congregants, the fear may arise from what we know all too well. We may have experienced how others who spoke unwelcome words were treated. We may not want to jeopardize relationships gifted and burdened with history, not to mention reciprocity (you scratch my back, and I'll scratch yours).

The subsequent stories of Jeremiah and the women who came to the tomb reveal that fear of others' reactions does have grounds for justification. When the women bring their witness to the disciples, how does Luke describe the result? "These words seemed to them an idle tale, and they did not believe them" (24:11). As for Jeremiah, his witness as prophet is met with disdain by the people and particularly the leaders to whom he directs it. Even more pronounced is the response by those closest to Jeremiah, as described in an oracle set in God's voice: "For even your kinsfolk and your own family, even they have dealt treacherously with you; they are in full cry after you" (12:6). Such fears may be justified, but are they productive? A seminary professor of mine once remarked, half jokingly yet half seriously, that just because you are paranoid doesn't mean that people aren't out to get you. It's just that paranoia is an unhealthy way of dealing with reality, much like letting fear of others control our lives. It's not that our anticipations or trepidations of others' reactions are unjustified, but giving in to such fear is unhealthy and unproductive

Such fear of others would have far less impact on us if deeper fears were not at work: our fears about ourselves. We may unduly fear others' nonacceptance, which leads us to invest their regard with far more influence over us than is merited. We may fear times of loneliness that have weighed us down in the past, which leads us to bend over backward to mollify others so as not to find ourselves on the outside looking in. We may fear that our words could reveal us for who we are—or who we are not.

To those deeper fears rooted not in others but in ourselves, God speaks: "Do not be afraid." Why? Because the gift of God's grace and unconditional acceptance disarms our fear of not being accepted. Because in the promise of God's presence, our fears of finding ourselves alone and isolated are met by One who stands by us and who assures us we belong. Or, to use the eloquent words of the Statement of Faith of the United Church of Canada: "In life, in death, in life beyond death, God is with us. We are not alone. Thanks be to God." Such acceptance, such belonging, enables us not to fear for ourselves or for others. Such acceptance, such belonging, forms the basis for our witness to a world driven by fear.

Witnesses in Time

Faithful witness takes place within a particular time and is offered to a particular situation. While that sounds simple, the implications and stakes are enormous. Consider, first, the example of the women at the tomb. The witness they are entrusted with is this: "'Go and tell my brothers to go to Galilee; there they will see me.'" The interpretations for *why* they need to go to Galilee to see Jesus are legion and have spawned all manner of sermons. I know, because I have preached some of them. But Matthew does not specify any of those reasons. The message, the witness, is simple: get to Galilee. It is a timely witness, one in need of heeding at that moment, because we all know the disciples and the eventual church did not stay in Galilee.

Faithful witness takes place within a particular time and is offered to a particular situation. Consider now Jeremiah, where matters get even more complicated. Why? Because over the course of the book of Jeremiah, the witness changes. Initially, the witness can be summed up as follows: get ready for judgment. "The prophets prophesy falsely, and the priests rule as the prophets direct; my people love to have it so" (5:31). But Jeremiah's witness does not stay on that one note. Over time, likely influenced by the devastating experience of exile, Jeremiah's witness shifts to: get ready for hope. "The people who survived the sword found grace in the wilderness" (31:2). Those who like things in neat packages and without contradictions might ask, "So, is it judgment or hope?" To which Jeremiah, like Isaiah, would bear witness: "both."

How can it be both? The witness depends upon the time and the situation. God's word to a community overly satisfied with itself in spite of glaring injustices conveniently overlooked will differ from the word offered to a community reeling from disaster and self-blame. Those two very different words belong to Jeremiah's original call to witness. Look at the final verse of this chapter's passage from Jeremiah and the verbs assigned to the witness of the prophet: pluck up and pull down, destroy and overthrow, build and plant. Witness relies on perceiving the need of those addressed for God's transforming presence and power. As the first four verbs make clear, sometimes that transformation necessitates deconstruction of ways that have strayed from covenant purposes of love and justice and compassion. But as the second two verbs, build and plant, make clear, that transformation sometimes calls for witness to God's restoration and renewal for the sake of that same covenant.

To offer witness to God's transforming power and presence, then, invites sensitivity to the timely needs of those addressed—including ourselves. It does no good to cry "go to Galilee" when Galilee's time has come and gone. It does even less good to witness to warnings of judgment after judgment has come—or to dwell on hope to those whose deeper need is to have things shaken up.

"Do not be afraid" offers an invitation not to fear the times into which we speak—and not to fear speaking the truth most needed in those times. That is an important invitation to keep in mind when we fear saying anything that could be heard as not comforting or supportive. That is an important invitation to keep in mind when we see our strongest suit as being a burr under the saddle of authority when what is most needed from us is encouragement and kindness.

Faithful witness requires remarkable flexibility on our part: flexibility that opens us to the witness God would make in this particular time and place. Some individuals and communities of faith struggle with such flexibility and perhaps even fear it. We grow comfortable, some might say static, with words and witness that worked in previous times in this place. Or perhaps we grow envious of words and witness that seem to work in other places in this time, and we end up trying on every new idea or program that somebody's cousins cited as effective at their church. Either way we are tempted to go merely with what is traditional or what is sold as practical—and not spend enough time discerning with

God and with others what truly is faithful witness in this time and in this place.

Our calling as witnesses invites us to practice discernment over faithfulness. Discerning the timely witness is not a matter of closing our eyes, opening the Bible, putting our finger on the page, and reading the verse. Discerning the witness that is timely is a matter of listening closely to God through scripture and community and listening closely to the needs of community and world. And once discerned, not fearing to speak in a timely fashion.

Witness and Not Living Afraid

In the best of all possible worlds, faith's witnesses could participate in a "witness protection program." You could freely speak your word in testimony to God's transforming power and know that if it created any waves you would be whisked away to a "safe house." There you could peaceably live in anonymity, free of reprisals from the powers that be—ecclesial, political, or social.

However, faith's witness is never anonymous because it comes from particular individuals and groups who live within and speak to particular locales and situations. As a result, faith's witness is never without risk; the goal is not safety but transformation. God does not give us false identities to disguise our voice or cloak who we truly are. God beckons us to trust the word of "do not be afraid" and then bids us speak as witnesses to the holy in life.

Is that enough for us to find our voice? Is that enough for us to offer timely witness? We answer those questions by the way we live and the words we speak that intentionally point to the God who is their source and hope. The women at the tomb so lived and so spoke, in spite of the initially chilly reaction they received. Jeremiah so lived and so spoke, even when times changed and with them the direction of Jeremiah's witness.

The times in which we live are full of change and ripe for witness. There is likely no more challenging need for our witness in these times than setting fear aside for the sake of bringing the transforming purposes of God to bear on issues of justice. The next chapter addresses that call to set aside fear and not live afraid for the sake of justice.

SPIRITUAL EXERCISE #1

Imagine what has sometimes been called the "elevator conversation." Only one other person is in the elevator, and he knows you go to church. With a thirty-second ride ahead, he asks, "Just why do you bother with that religion stuff?"

- Given the thirty-second window, what will you say and why will you say it?
- What will make it true to you as opposed to something this person can read in a book?

Try this exercise now. Say what is most true to your life and experience of God.

Pray for God's guidance and gift of not being afraid in the "windows" that occur for your witness.

SPIRITUAL EXERCISE #2

Recall how this chapter spoke earlier of a witness as one inserted between God and others.

- Who served as faith's witness for you?
- What did they say or do that revealed God's presence and love to you?

Consider where and how God might "insert" you as a witness.

- Who might look to you for faith's witness?
- What fears might hold you back?

Pray for God's help to serve as a witness when the time and place is right. Be strengthened in the reminder that witness does not draw attention to self but to God.

SPIRITUAL EXERCISE #3

Think of a favorite hymn or song of yours that has "witness" for its theme. Reflect on how the words in that hymn depict witness: its motive, its scope, its power.

- When and where have you exemplified its celebration of witness?
- What fears have held you back from living its affirmations of witness?

Name those fears, one at a time. After each one, repeat God's word to you: "do not be afraid."

Prayerfully seek God's help in bringing "do not be afraid" into present opportunities for witness.

SPIRITUAL EXERCISE #4

Consider the times in which you live: in your life, in your congregation, in the world.

Focus on one pressing and timely matter that cries out for faith's witness.

- What word and/or action of witness seems most needed, most timely, to you?
- What part might you play in bringing that witness to bear, alone or with others?

Pray for God's guidance for how to best carry out that witness.

Open yourself to the Spirit's leading in freeing your voice and life to bear witness. This day, this week, give that witness as God calls and Spirit empowers you.

6

For the Sake of Justice

ZECHARIAH 8:11-17
1 PETER 3:13-17

IN 1845 THE AMERICAN POET and abolitionist James Russell Lowell published an eighteen-stanza poem titled "The Present Crisis." Initially written in opposition to the war with Mexico that Lowell feared would extend the borders of slavery, the poem took on greater meaning as the nation moved toward civil war. Some of its lines found their way into the following hymn:

> Once to every man and nation comes the moment to decide,
> In the strife of truth with falsehood, for the good or evil side;
> Some great cause, God's new Messiah, offering each the bloom
>   or blight,
> And the choice goes by forever 'twixt that darkness and
>   that light.
> . . . .
> Though the cause of evil prosper, yet 'tis truth alone is
>   strong,
> Truth forever on the scaffold, wrong forever on the throne.
> Yet that scaffold sways the future, and, behind the dim
>   unknown,
> Standeth God within the shadow keeping watch above His own.[5]

Several Web sites note that "Once to Every Man and Nation" has not made it into many modern hymnals in the United States.

73

Some attribute that to inclusive language difficulties. Others suggest the omission stems from theological fine points: surely more than one point of decision in our lives exists, and what's this about a new Messiah?

However, the hymn's language remains striking, especially when sung to its traditional pairing with the moving Welsh tune TON-Y-BOTEL (EBENEZER). And the hymn's theme cuts across the ages. One of the Web sites related the story of a D-day commemoration service in England. The planner of the service, having no personal memories of the event, spoke to an individual who took part in the landing. That individual suggested a hymn for the ceremony that he had learned as an English schoolboy: "Once to Every Man and Nation." I remember singing these words in my youth during the 1960s; the hymn provided strong connections between my still-developing faith and the issues of justice at stake in the civil rights movement in the United States.

This chapter takes up the issue of justice and the setting aside of fears so that we might do what is just and right. This hymn, and even more so the poem that preceded it, exposes where such fear might arise. Scaffolded truth and enthroned wrong admit that justice must sometimes contend with skewed systems of power. One of the hymn's lines speaks of "the light of burning martyrs." That harsh and repelling image is by no means a false one when it comes to what justice-making risks when wrong is enthroned.

But the hymn raises the timeliness and decisiveness that justice always involves. While we face choices and opportunities for justice more than once in our lives, some of those opportunities and the decisions they invite us to make do have a time that comes and goes. Acting for justice cannot always afford to wait until all is settled, clear, and obvious. In truth, justice can rarely afford such leisure when right is at stake in a critical moment. Our scripture passages from the prophet Zechariah and an epistle attributed to Peter inform our setting fear aside for the sake of justice. Each passage brings an urging to do right and to do good, even as both speak out of circumstances that might otherwise have elicited fear.

Justice and the Purposes of God

To some, the linking of justice with the purposes of God may sound like an innovation of the modern church, sometimes associated with late-nineteenth-century's "social gospel movement." Worse yet, in other narratives, that joining of social with gospel is vilified as the cause for decline in what formerly were known as mainline churches in the 1950s and 1960s. Aren't the losses in membership and churches of those church traditions traceable to involvement in civil rights and Vietnam war protests, and later on women's rights and the gay/lesbian issues?

I am not a church sociologist, so I leave the deciphering of such explanations to those armed with longitudinal studies of church trends. But what I do know is that linking justice and God's purposes is not a late-nineteenth-century invention. The evangelical who penned the words of the much-beloved "Amazing Grace" did so in repentance of his years as a slave-ship captain. He later wrote a tract in 1787 to support the abolitionist campaign led by a young William Wilberforce. Far earlier, a Christian monk named Telemachus so opposed the practice of gladiatorial contests that he intervened in one at the cost of his own life. Tradition holds that, in response, the Roman emperor Honorius issued an edict banning such contests.

Such stories as these, however, barely scratch the antiquity of the link between justice and God's purposes. Luke's Gospel is keen on this connection. Luke's narration of the ministry of John the Baptizer includes explicit words about sharing goods with those in need, along with ethical guidelines for vocations noted for abuses (Luke 3:10-14). Even more telling is Luke's story of Jesus' ministry in Nazareth (Luke 4:16-21). Jesus reads words from Isaiah that speak of good news to the poor, release to the captives, healing of the

75

blind, freedom for those oppressed, and the proclamation of the year of God's favor—a veiled reference to the radical social practices associated with Jubilee (Lev. 25). To punctuate these practices of justice with his own ministry, Jesus declares the fulfilling of these words not in some promised future time but *today*.

The association of the doing of justice with God's purposes goes even further back. Leviticus, that mostly dry-as-dust collection of cultic laws governing ritual practices often alien to our experience, insists on the pairing of social justice with righteousness. It commands the leaving of gleanings in your field for the poor—which is to say, not to be so absorbed by profit that you forget your neighbor's need. It counsels that nobody is to tinker with weights and measures to gain unjust advantage in the marketplace—which is to say, no insider trading.

Why all of this detail about God's purposes for justice? To borrow a phrase sometimes used in efforts to separate justice from relationship with God: if we are to practice the old-time religion, we had better get it old enough. Old enough as eighteenth- and nineteenth-century evangelicals who did not bat an eye at combining traditional faith with untraditional and controversial campaigns against slavery. Old enough as Jesus' "just as you did it to one of the least of these who are members of my family, you did it to me" (Matt. 25:40). Old enough as Amos's "let justice roll down like waters and righteousness like an ever-flowing stream" (5:24).

Does linking justice with God's purposes risk the status quo for us? Absolutely. Amos was told to go back to his home. John the Baptizer was beheaded. Rome executed Jesus for the threat posed to civil order by one heralded as a "king" and thus rival to Caesar. Several U.S. denominations split into northern and southern bodies before the Civil War, rifts not healed until well into the twentieth century. Why take such risks for justice? Justice and the purposes of God cannot be separated. "Do not be afraid" is the encouragement God brings, the word God offers, to do what is right and good and just. Justice *is* the old-time purpose of God.

A Rhetorical Question?

Several Bible verses and various folk proverbs speak of good being rewarded by good. But perhaps you have also heard the phrase, "no good deed goes unpunished." It seems a rather cynical word. Why would good be punished, and by whom? The answer provided by history too often is this: whenever and by whomever justice is feared. Examples abound. Those in Europe who sought to hide Jews from the Nazis risked suffering the fate of those for whom they acted. Whistle-blowers today who disclose unjust or unsafe workplace practices have sometimes found themselves without a job or future in their chosen field of work.

So the question in 1 Peter 3:13 of "who will harm you if you are eager to do what is good?" is not a rhetorical question that presumes the answer will always and everywhere be "no one." The very next verse strongly implies that truth: "but even if you do suffer for doing what is right. . . ." Doing what is right can bring suffering. The community addressed by First Peter is acknowledged to have known this truth firsthand because of persecution. The Greek verb *pascho* ("to suffer") occurs eleven times in this brief letter, almost the number of times it is used in all of the Gospels combined. This community is well acquainted with the results of abuse of power and justice denied. Yet the author counsels the community not to fear those who may inflict suffering, not to allow negative outcomes in the short run to deter their eagerness to do good. Justice cannot become a slave to "what's in it for me," especially when immediate outcomes make it appear that doers of justice inevitably go punished.

This possibility makes First Peter's word of "do not fear" all the more compelling. For consider: if the doing of good brought only accolades, what's to fear? The encouragement to "do not fear" is aimed toward the circumstances that bring conflict and risk to those who would do what is right and just and good in this world. Go back to that question raised at the passage's beginning: "who will harm you if you are eager to do what is good?" The answer points to those who stand to lose if good is done or justice is upheld. The answer points to those who stand to lose if rights are no longer denied and the disenfranchised are given voice. The answer points to those who stand to lose if the earth is no longer viewed as ours to pollute and deplete as we please with no thought to future generations. The answer points to those who stand to lose if their worldviews are not lauded as the final word.

The question raised by First Peter also contains a clue as to what it means not to live afraid for the sake of justice: "*eager* to do what is good" (emphasis added). Eager translates the word *zelotes*. Zealot. Eagerness does not simply entail an energetic attitude brought to a task. The sense of this word involves a single-minded pursuit of a goal. That goal, in this case, is the doing of good. Yet how do we sometimes hear or use the word "do-gooder"? More often than not it is employed as a slur: someone who wants to change us, usually someone with an overly high opinion of self.

There is some truth in that. The doing of good, the working of justice, is indeed about bringing change. That's the part that entails risk. And by necessity, the doing of what is right and just comes attached to an overly high opinion, but it is not of oneself. Justice is sought precisely because of the high opinion God has for its doing and, in turn, our high opinion of the One who calls us to do good. The other high opinion involved regards those for whose sake justice is sought: typically the ones that folks resistant to justice look down their noses upon. To do justice for and with the poor, the vulnerable, the ones currently out of public favor, values them for who and for whose they are: children of God. We share with them that same identity. We seek justice for and with them as their equals, not their betters. We seek to do justice, not for the reward it may or may not bring but for the God whose covenant seeks good to be done for the sake of God's holy purposes.

FOR THE SAKE OF JUSTICE

"These Are the Things That You Shall Do"

At one time students of preaching were taught to avoid the language of "must" and "ought" in sermons. I know, because that was the case in the years of my own seminary education. I can understand the purpose of that counsel. Sermons ought (oops!)— sermons are to invite and persuade folks, not dictate nonnegotiable terms to them. Viewed from another angle, the preacher who continually places self in the role of saying what must or ought to be done by others subtly assumes the place of God or lawgiver for the listeners. And are we not about grace? Is faith not a decision of free will made by the individual, a decision that cannot be coerced or short-circuited by another? I understand that.

I also understand and believe that some things are to be done and some are not. A colleague of mine, the Rev. Dr. Marie Fortune of the FaithTrust Institute of Seattle, has dedicated much of her ministry to preventing clergy abuse of parishioners. In the past, some of the boundary lines have been ill-defined, especially for those new to ministry. I recall a story Marie told about being invited to address a group of seminarians, some of whom would soon be set loose into the field of pastoral ministry. One of the claims of pastors who have stumbled or connived their way into situations involving abuse was that "no one ever told me that was wrong." So Marie, in addressing those seminarians, placed this before them: "Taking advantage of a parishioner, crossing boundaries, especially sexual boundaries, is wrong and unethical. Now, don't ever say you've never been told!" Knowing her, I am sure my colleague was far more eloquent and addressed the issue in much greater detail in her words. But the bottom line is this: such conduct is never right. It must not be done. Period.

What is true of pastors in that specific issue broadens into conduct for us all as children of God and disciples of Jesus. There just are some things that are to be done, and some that are not. What things form the core of what constitutes justice?

The title of this section, "These Are the Things That You Shall Do," comes from Zechariah 8:16. Zechariah came later than the prophetic works gathered in the books of Isaiah, Jeremiah, and Ezekiel. Zechariah spoke to those who had returned from exile to rebuild Jerusalem and the Temple—sometime after the rebuilding had begun but before the Temple had been completed. Zechariah addressed the changed circumstances of the former exiles and how this reflected a transformation in God's purposes from bringing disaster to doing good. But even in the midst of this amazing shift, to which God speaks "do not be afraid," Zechariah went on to tell of what had not changed. What remained the same in that day, as in the much earlier days of Isaiah and Jeremiah and back further to Amos and Micah, was the call to do justice.

Listen again to Zechariah's litany of what the returned exiles were to do: speak the truth to one another; render judgments (the word can also be translated "justice") in the public places that make for peace; do not make plans for evil against one another; do not love false oaths. These were the commands that had been consistent from the days of the early prophets. These were the commands that those earlier prophets drew upon from the prior covenant stipulations of Sinai. Some things don't change—and the need to do justice is one of them.

The timing of Zechariah's words about what we are to do (and not do) is compelling in a country undergoing reconstruction. Its symbols of society and worship, the wall and the Temple, were being rebuilt. Yet even as that rebuilding progressed, Zechariah urged an even more critical reconstruction: the reconstruction of justice that honored God's ancient purposes for covenanted relationship with neighbor and stranger.

As much as things change, things stay the same. Spiritual renewal, whether of individuals or religious communities, is a lively task in our day. Such renewal can rightly be viewed as a reconstruction of our relationship with God. Books like the one you now read have such renewal as their purpose. But spiritual renewal in any form is empty unless it partners with the doing of justice. In Zechariah's time, people emphasized the physical rebuilding of institutions and a resumption of rituals of worship at the Temple that exile had interrupted. But when the prophet singled out the priorities of what must be done in the midst of this reconstruction, works of justice came to the forefront. In our time, when we would renew our spirituality and invigorate the life of our faith communities, that word still holds true. Zechariah's priorities remain ours: speak truth, render justice, make for peace, devise good rather than evil plans, love no false oath. And as Zechariah might have said in his day had he heard Dr. Fortune addressing those seminarians: "Now, don't ever say you've never been told!"

Justice and Not Living Afraid

This chapter began with stanzas from the hymn "Once to Every Man and Nation." So it is fitting to bring this chapter to a close with other lines from that hymn, words that speak and sing the ongoing challenge of not living afraid for the sake of doing justice:

> New occasions teach new duties, time makes ancient good
> uncouth;
> They must upward still and onward, who would keep
> abreast of truth.

While God's purposes for justice never change, the situations in which those purposes must be lived out continually shift. In the story of Telemachus mentioned earlier, his stand against gladiatorial contests was a bold witness to God's justice. Gladiatorial contests are no longer a pressing justice issue for twenty-first century Christians. We have new occasions to address with new duties of justice. Likewise, to say we oppose slavery in the United States is a gesture long past its moment of decision and risk. The tentacles of racism that persist from that era, however, provide very timely challenges for justice work today.

To choose not to live afraid in the face of such issues means we do not shy away from confronting present needs for justice. We do not do so, even when people content with things as they are would "shush" justice ministries for fear of losing members and support. Why? Justice, the doing of what is right and good, is not a secondary concern of God that lags behind keeping peace in the pews and tenure in the pulpit. Justice, the doing of what is right and good, goes to the heart of God's purposes not only for the church but for all creation. The life and mission to which God bids us not to live afraid seeks transformation that encompasses individuals and communities of faith and on to societies and the whole of creation. Such transformation will form the theme for this book's seventh and final chapter.

SPIRITUAL EXERCISE #1

Read aloud the opening stanza of "Once to Every Man and Nation" (page 73). Recall a decision you faced or a stand you took in your own life around some issue of justice.

- What made this issue and decision compelling for you?
- In what ways did fear(s) play a role in your decision (or struggle) to take a stand?
- Then, and now: how does the issue of justice relate to your faith priorities?

Consider the ways this decision and stand have impacted you.

Pray for God's guidance in such issues and decisions regarding justice you face today.

SPIRITUAL EXERCISE #2

Write a journal entry that reflects on these questions:

- What do you understand to be God's chief purposes for your life and church?
- How do these purposes intersect with matters of justice?
- Write underneath your entry: "Do not be afraid, and do not live afraid."
- Where among those purposes do you and/or your church struggle with fears, and why?

Identify one particular fear that holds you and your church back from those purposes.

Pray that God's Spirit will help you release that fear so that you can better keep faith with that purpose.

SPIRITUAL EXERCISE #3

Consider an individual or group in your community for whom justice has been denied or for whom good has not been rewarded

DO NOT LIVE AFRAID

but seemingly punished. In what ways might you speak or even act on their behalf, if not to restore justice then at least to stand with them with compassion?

Determine to perform one action in the coming week that expresses your solidarity with the individual or group, no matter how small or insignificant it may seem to you.

Pray for God's help to perform one action . . . and see where it and God may lead you.

SPIRITUAL EXERCISE #4

List no more than five fundamental values that guide your life. How did you come to own these values as guides for your life and relationships? What makes them "nonnegotiables" for you?

Prayerfully consider how this list reflects your faith commitments.

- Where do you see God's priority of justice reflected in these values?
- For each value, what fears have you faced in seeking to live by them?

Pray for God's ongoing transformation of your values with the justice and grace of God.

7

For the Sake of Transformation

GENESIS 50:15-21
MATTHEW 17:1-7

I FIRST HEARD MYRA WELCH'S POEM "The Touch of the Master's Hand" on the late 1980s version of *The Smothers Brothers Comedy Hour*. When the actor started reciting it, I thought he was going to spoof the poem's archaic language. He did not. Instead, he let the words movingly tell their story of an old violin put up for auction. The bidding goes nowhere on the "battered and scarred" instrument until a stranger steps forward. He takes the violin in his hands, dusts it off, does a bit of tuning, and begins to play music that is, in the words of the poem, as "sweet as a caroling angel sings." The stranger then sets the violin down, and the auction resumes. Only now, instead of bids that balk at three dollars, the offers reach three thousand dollars. The difference? That would be the meaning of the poem's title. What went perceived as a thing without worth became precious. The transformation in this instance was not of the violin itself. It already held that potential. The violin only needed someone to reveal its beauty and worth. Transformation resulted.

Transformation can itself evoke fear. We become accustomed to things and people as they are. We may not always be happy or satisfied with our status quos: in relationships with others, in understandings or assumptions about ourselves, perhaps even in our rapport with God. But we sometimes reason, better the devil we know than the one we don't. So we attempt to maintain things and others as they are. As we are.

Transformation poses a threat to such suppositions, for transformation implies that things around us and things within us need not stay as they are. Possibilities for change exist. Transformation may come, as in the poem, through altered perceptions. If I realize, for example, that I do not have to view the Muslim or right-wing fundamentalist as an enemy, that other does not undergo change. Transformation comes in my perception of them. Transformation may also move beyond perceptions of the world into acknowledgments that things and persons, ourselves included, can change substantially. One of the Bible stories this chapter will explore is that of Jesus' transfiguration. This story is more than the disciples' perceiving Jesus in a new light. Jesus himself changes, setting the stage for the disciples being beckoned not to be afraid.

Setting fear aside for the sake of transformation serves as this final chapter's theme, even as its theme provides the decisive bridge between this book and your life. Spiritual growth that takes root and endures comes from our transformation at the hands of God. The story of Jesus' transfiguration and the narrative of Joseph with his brothers will offer insights into the ways of fear-freed transformation. But their stories and others like them in the biblical witness can only provide glimpses and precedents of such change. Our own transformation awaits our opening to the intentions of God in our day and for our lives. Our transformation relies upon finding wholeness and courage from Christ's healing and uplifting touch, which bids us to fearlessness as we move into the future in company with the Spirit and people of God.

Opening to God's Intentions

A prayer common among various liturgical traditions is this: "Forgive what we have been, amend what we are, direct what we shall be." The words of this prayer relate directly to what it means to

FOR THE SAKE OF TRANSFORMATION

open ourselves to the transformation that is both God's intention and gift for our lives. The story of Joseph and his brothers serves as a parable of such regeneration at work when fear is set aside.

The brothers fear for their lives, presuming that Joseph will act toward them exactly as they once acted toward him when they cast him into a pit and then sold him into slavery. While their words beg forgiveness, it is a forgiveness that carries the baggage of the past. All they can do when they approach Joseph is to throw themselves before him as slaves, in the hope they will be more valuable to Joseph alive than dead. What their fear does not account for is the transformation that forgiveness can generate. For Joseph, forgiveness of what has been, in terms of his brothers' previous actions, is already accomplished. Because of that, Joseph is in a position to amend the present circumstances of his brothers from groveling to embracing. And out of that amending of the present situation, Joseph opens up the future of what shall be for his kin—from fearing his reprisal to ones enjoying his providence.

We can also experience this providence by opening ourselves to God's transforming purposes. The role of forgiveness in transformation is paramount. Change will come grudgingly, if at all, so long as we are held captive to our pasts, whether those captivities be to sins we have committed (or omitted) *or* to the sins of others that we will not dismiss. In either case, *what has been* will block efforts to change *what is* and *what still can be*. Transformation hinges on our ability to be set free from elements in our past that would otherwise enslave us. We feel wounded by another, and the wound takes on a life—or death—all its own if not confronted and released. We feel ourselves a failure in some moment in our lives and find ourselves unable to let that one failure go until its influence multiplies and poisons our entire view of self. The inability to forgive or to accept forgiveness stands as a significant hurdle to positive change in our lives.

The gift of forgiveness, both in its receiving and in its offering, forms God's liberating intention for our lives, freeing us from past mistakes. Only then may we move forward to the amending "what we are" part of the prayer and into the future. With forgiveness, everything is open for change. The truth of that surfaces in far more than personal and family relationships in need of renewal and restoration. Consider, for example, the work of the Truth and Reconciliation Commission in South Africa following the dismantling of apartheid. It gave opportunity for victims to air injustices endured and for oppressors to confess complicity in violence and request amnesty. While not a perfect system, in the end, it helped that nation move beyond a horrific past into the future.

In the Joseph narrative, the future is directed into life-giving rather than life-threatening ways when Joseph promises he will provide not only for those who once harmed him but for their children as well. The exercise of a single individual's forgiveness unleashes transformation for the good of coming generations. Seen in that light, Joseph's example opens up the dramatic possibilities of what such transformation may bring to our lives and to those around us. Joseph's choice to act on the basis of forgiveness transforms an entire community.

Now you and I may think we do not have such possibilities placed before us. We may presume that most of our choices about whether we will exercise or accept forgiveness has little if any effect beyond ourselves. But the Joseph story suggests otherwise. Every single act that opens to the transforming purposes of God has untold possibilities. We may not see them all ahead of time. We may be unaware of how one decision ripples out to affect the lives of others in the short- and long-term. But our awareness does not limit the ability of God to bring good. Remember how Joseph phrased his reply to the brothers? Their original intention to do harm was met by God's intention to do good.

So imagine when our intentions to do good encounter God's intentions to do good. Who knows what may happen! Who knows how many lives may be transformed by the decision to open ourselves and our world to the good God intends and the forgiveness Christ offers. So have no fear to trust God's forgiving of what you have been, God's amending of who you are, and God's directing of who you are still in the process of becoming. In every one of those actions we are being transformed by nothing less than the grace and love of God for us and all creation.

Whose Transfiguration?

Transfiguration is the word Matthew and Mark use to describe what happens to (in?) Jesus on a high mountain. But what exactly does transfiguration mean? The Greek word used by Matthew and Mark is *metamorphoo,* from which we get the English "metamorphosis." In biology, metamorphosis denotes a radical change in structure during growth, such as a caterpillar's "morphing" into a butterfly or a tadpole into a frog. In geology, metamorphosis defines dramatic change in rock forms brought about by heat and/or pressure. So Matthew and Mark's use of this word in reference to what happens to Jesus on the mountain points to an act of transformation that goes far deeper than the outward signs of shining face and dazzling clothes. On the mountain, Jesus is transformed, the exact nature of which remains a mystery. But the transformation on this mountain does not end with Jesus.

A voice from heaven intones words spoken about Jesus at his baptism, adding to them the injunction: "listen to him!" With that, the disciples fall to the ground, "overcome by fear." Fear cast the brothers of Joseph down on the ground before him, when they saw no alternative but to offer themselves as slaves for what they perceived as the only hope of saving their necks. Fear even earlier caused Abraham to lie intentionally about the identity of Sarah as his sister rather than wife, presuming the truth would result in his murder by an envious king. Fear can do such things in our lives. Fear can paralyze us, freezing us in positions and attitudes that we may not want but for which we see no alternative. Fear can cast palls of silence over us when we become afraid to speak the truth. Fear brings us to our knees when we might seem too much of a target if we stand up straight, literally or ethically.

It is more than curious that Jesus' transformation on the mountain does not throw the disciples down on the ground in fear. Neither does the appearance of Moses and Elijah. Fear comes when the voice affirms Jesus' identity and the necessity to listen to him. Why might that induce fear? Context. The narrative immediately preceding the Transfiguration story in Matthew is Jesus' teaching of the cross for the first time. That teaching speaks not only of Jesus' impending suffering, death, and raising in Jerusalem. It also includes Jesus' declaration that if any would be followers, they are to take up their own crosses. What crashes the disciples down to the ground in fear is not Jesus' transformation but the possibility of their own. The voice that commands "listen to him" summons obedience to the one who calls them to the way of the cross.

At times we still scramble for ground cover in fear when the summons to transformation comes our way. In our churches, we may admit the need for renewal and redevelopment but fear what that will mean for favored ways of doing things. In our families and friendships, we may recognize relationships need improvement but fear resisting the admission of our being part of the problem or our changing part of the solution. In our faith, we may offer confessions of "forgive us" more readily than invocations of "amend us" for fear of having to let go of what we still deep down are comfortable hanging on to. After all, next week's confession of sin for absolution may take less work than this week's opening to transformation.

On the mountain, Jesus' transformation remains largely a matter of mystery. On the mountain, the disciples' fear of transformation is no mystery at all. They fall to the ground, overwhelmed by fear. But the One who seeks transformation for would-be followers does not leave them there. Which is to say, the One who seeks transformation does not leave *us* there.

Rising Up and Moving On

The power of human touch can be extraordinary—for good or ill. The emphasis paid these days on instructing our children on the difference between "good touch" and "bad touch" grows out of the tragic abuse of human touch against vulnerable ones. Violence, sexual or otherwise, perverts the gift of touch. But sometimes, in our understandable eagerness to find shelter from touch that abuses or takes advantage of or just plain feels wrong, we may isolate ourselves from the potential for touch that nurtures and shelters and just plain does good. My wife carries a vivid memory of her childhood pastor whose large hands would gently but firmly envelop hers at the door of the church after worship. For her, those hands and that touch became a tactile sign of the safety and well-being she experienced in Christian community.

Matthew frames the turning point in the Transfiguration story between Jesus' transformation and the disciples' own path of transformation with these words: "Jesus came and touched them." As they lay on the ground, fearful, Jesus does not withdraw but comes to them. Jesus touches them. That touch serves as prelude to the invitation most needed at that moment: "'Get up and do not be afraid.'" Two intriguing details emerge in this portion of the passage. First, in Matthew's Gospel, every other occurrence of this verb "to touch" is used in a healing story. "Healing touch" is no figure of speech in Matthew. Touch routinely restores wholeness. Second, the verb translated as "get up" is the same verb used elsewhere in reference to resurrection.

Taken together, these details further deepen the meaning of this scene and where "do not be afraid" intends to lead. We are not left by ourselves to will up the resolve to fear no longer. The ability to set aside fear comes from the experience of Jesus' healing and empowering touch in our lives. Christ comes to us, as Christ came to those disciples, in moments of fear not to point accusing fingers but to enfold us in strong hands. Perhaps even more telling, the call to set fear aside is implicitly linked in this passage by the call to "get up" and move on. It is not clear whether the disciples make the connection between this call to "get up" and Jesus' use of this same verb in the previous chapter's teaching on the cross and being "raised up" (16:21). But the community to whom Matthew wrote would likely have recognized the link between the promise of Jesus "raised up" and the disciples now called to "get up." With Matthew's community, we find ourselves called and empowered to rise above fear by the promise of resurrection. Like those disciples of old, we are called to get up and be on our God-transformed way in the service of the resurrected Christ who journeys with us.

Jesus touches our lives in healing and empowering ways that free us from fear to go and do likewise in the way we live toward and for others. It is worth remembering that, in the middle of the Transfiguration story, Peter offers to build three dwellings on top of the mountain for Jesus, Moses, and Elijah. One can read between the lines the hope that the disciples could also stay there and bask in the light of Jesus' transformation, far away from crowds that prove fickle and authorities that prove fatal. Jesus turns down the request. His own transformation complete, the story leads down off the mountain toward ministry that will shape the disciples' and the world's transformation.

Spiritual life and transformation are not ultimately about staying on spiritual mountaintops, reveling in moments of holy encounter that isolate us from the worries of the world. Spiritual life and transformation are ultimately about coming down off the mountain and living the transformed life in places where fear runs rampant and love is in short supply. The touch of Jesus, extended through the most human of hands and ministries, can still bring healing and restoration in those places. God's power to transform life, to bring good out of intended harm, even to bring life out of death, bids us let go of our fears and move on with the way of Christ.

Transformation and Not Living Afraid

Throughout this book we have explored God's gospel word of "do not be afraid" and how it breaks open the possibilities for key movements in our spiritual journeys. Trust, vocation, witness, justice, and transformation: our lives in these areas are set free by that invitation to no longer live afraid. The invitation is extended simply in word alone. Jesus' life and ministry offer a lived example of that "not fearing." The presence of the Spirit who accompanies us now gives us support, guidance, and strength in the challenging moments that remain before us.

Note also that fearlessness is not, in the language and experience of faith, a synonym for recklessness. Reckless lives have no regard for the future. They careen from one high risk to another. Fearless lives, as this book and these readings have underscored, live with absolute regard for the future. The future, no longer feared as an ominous unknown, is trusted as the ultimate dominion of God's love.

This book ends where it began: with the affirmation of God's love and that love's invitation of our trust to negate the power of fear. Have we not gone in a rather large circle? Clearly, the answer is yes. When it comes to the nature of God's power to transform our lives for the good, love is the final word . . . even as trust opens us to God's love. Love cannot be coerced or grounded in fear, as the opening chapter's reference to 1 John 4:18-19 makes abundantly clear. For us to open to the love of God, fear must give way to trust. In that opening through trust and in that gift that is God's love comes our transformation.

So do not be afraid: of God, of the future, of our transformation in Christ.

What God seeks is our good.

What God offers is love incarnate.

Trust these things—and do not live afraid!

SPIRITUAL EXERCISE #1

Recall a moment, an experience, where your outlook on another person changed substantially. In what ways did that transformation in perspective arise out of change you saw in that person? In what ways did that transformation of perspective arise out of change in yourself?

Find and read the poem "The Touch of the Master's Hand" (accessible on the Internet).

- What times in your life might you have identified with the violin in that poem?
- Who served as the stranger in that poem for you and in what words or actions?

Prayerfully consider someone whose value and worth you might affirm in the name of Christ.

SPIRITUAL EXERCISE #2

Offer the following prayer, one petition for each section of the prayer, then repeating the cycle.

Forgive what we have been.

What one thing from your past do you need to ask and/or offer forgiveness for?

Amend what we are.

How might receiving and/or offering that gift of forgiveness transform your life today?

Direct what we shall be.

Open yourself in hope to the newness God brings through this forgiving and amending.

SPIRITUAL EXERCISE #3

Remember your thoughts and feelings generated by the previous spiritual exercise. What fears of the need for forgiving, amending, or directing your life could you have experienced?

- Make a list of these fears on the left side of a sheet of paper.

- On the right side of the paper, alongside each fear, write one element or resource of faith that you can draw on to face that fear.

- Read aloud each fear coupled with the faith resource to face it, and then say, "Do not be afraid."

Observe a time of silence, holding in gratitude these gifts of faith to set aside fear.

SPIRITUAL EXERCISE #4

Imagine yourself on the mountaintop with Jesus. Be mindful of the matters that most concern you today: cares, hopes, fears, callings. In the midst of all these things, you feel the touch of Jesus upon your shoulder.

- What could Jesus say that would let you know of his compassion for you?

- What could Jesus say that would set you free from the fears that hold you back from life?

Listen as Jesus says those very things to you in word and in healing touch. Be at peace on your journey—and, in Christ, do not live afraid!

Leader's Guide

Introduction

THE FOLLOWING PAGES are for leaders who will use this book in a small-group setting. On the following facing pages is a template you can copy to plan each of the sessions. Space is provided on the template so that the copies will have room for you to make notes on the activities and exercises you choose to include in each session. The pages after the template contain suggestions and options for you to consider for each of the sessions you plan. The study can be done in seven sessions—eight, if you choose to include the optional introductory session. If you do not use the introductory session, please distribute the books a minimum of one week ahead of the first session with clear instructions to read the first chapter and do the spiritual exercises at the end of the chapter prior to the first session. The "Using This Book" section (page 11) provides guidance for how the reading and exercises can be done over the course of each week.

Hopefully, the template outline will provide flexibility in planning the sessions around your group's needs and interests. You are encouraged to incorporate the activities and exercises suggested here with your own ideas for engaging the chapter and spiritual exercises for each session.

The sessions are based on a 45-minute time period. If you have more (or less) time available, flex the suggested times below as needed: Gathering (5–10 minutes); Reflecting (15–20 minutes); Responding (10–15 minutes); Blessing and Commissioning (5–10 minutes).

Session Template

Session Focus

Preparation

Meeting space and worship center

Materials needed

Gathering

Welcome and introductions

Ritual

Entering the theme

Permission is granted to copy this page © 2009 Upper Room Books

Reflecting

Biblical background

Chapter review

Responding

Inward

Outward

Blessing and Commissioning

Review

Sending

Optional Introductory Session

To introduce the book, the guide for the readings and spiritual exercises, and the group process

Preparation

Cover a small table with colored cloths suggesting the hues of a rainbow. Place a candle on the table along with matches and/or lighter.

Materials needed: Bibles and copies of *Do Not Live Afraid* for each participant; two sheets of newsprint, one titled "Fear" and the other titled "Faith"; marking pens, materials for a large collage (large sheet of newsprint or poster board, pictorial magazines, glue sticks, marking pens, other art supplies)

Gathering

Welcome the participants. As people gather, invite them to write words or phrases they associate with the titles on the two sheets of posted newsprint. The artistically inclined might create a picture or image for that word. Once everyone is present, ask participants to read (view) the responses on the newsprint and to add others that may come to mind now. Suggest that the participants make connections between items listed on each: where do they complement each other, where do they contradict each other? What do those newsprint sheets suggest about the relationship between fear and faith?

Form a circle around or in front of the worship center. Light the candle. Call attention to the cloths or linens on the table. Ask participants to reflect on what those colors call to mind and heart. Indicate that, besides the reflections on those colors shared already, the cloths on the table invite remembrance of the rainbow. Read Genesis 9:8-17.

Note that while "do not be afraid" is not spoken overtly in the text, the passage is all about God's invitation for us not to live afraid. The bow in the clouds offers the promise of God's "never again" to the destruction of the Flood, a promise intended to free the characters in that story and us from having to fear the future. It is in God's hands. God will remember; the rainbow signals that remembrance. State that the colored cloths will be used on the worship center throughout this study to symbolize God's promise that we need not live in fear. Offer a prayer of thanks for that promise and for God's presence in this gathering and those to come, as we seek to open ourselves to God's assuring gift that we need not be afraid or live afraid.

Reflecting

Distribute copies of *Do Not Live Afraid*, if you have not done so already. Turn to "Using This Book" on page 11 and read together the opening two paragraphs. Invite responses, comments, or questions to the material. Allow time for discussion.

Read over the third and fourth paragraphs in "Using This Book" that summarize the structure of the book and the chapter contents. Indicate that each of the chapters lists scripture references. Encourage participants to read those texts prior to reading the chapter, as they will form part of each chapter's consideration of its theme. Turn to the "Spiritual Exercises" for chapter 1 that begin on page 23. Explain that each chapter has a set of four spiritual exercises.

Offer the following as the recommended pattern for each week's engagement of the materials. Day One: Read the chapter. Day Two: Do exercise #1. Day Three: Do exercise #2. Day Four: Do exercise #3. Day Five: Do exercise #4. Day Six: a weekly sabbath with no assignment, time for reflection. Day Seven: group session. Some individuals may want to adjust this by having the sabbath fall on the day after the session rather than before. Encourage the participants to pace themselves rather than cramming the chapter and daily exercises into one day. Spreading them over the course of the week will allow more time for the material and reflections on it to move deeper into their thinking and hearts. Invite those who have gone through similar studies to offer their thoughts and experiences.

Finally, have participants turn to the Leader's Guide materials (page 97). If the group will be rotating leadership, explain to those who will be sharing in the responsibilities that this will be their resource for planning. Clarify that you (and other leaders) are free to adapt the material to fit your group both in terms of interests and size.

Look over the "Session Template" (pages 98–99). Note that this basic structure will be used throughout these sessions. While the template primarily assists the leader(s) in planning, it also gives participants an understanding of the direction and flow of the meetings. Affirm, even if you have already done so, the importance of doing the readings and exercises for each session's chapter *prior to* the session. The session does not introduce the chapter content but takes us deeper into the material in company with one another and with the Spirit's leading through the group experience.

Responding

Ask participants to look at the book's cover. In what ways does that image speak to the need and gift of not living afraid? Suggest that group members reflect on the discussion from the GATHERING time that centered around the newsprint responses and the conversation about fear and faith. Invite participants to draw connections between the words and images on the newsprint sheets to situations in their church or wider community.

Encourage the group to focus on one situation in particular. How might these biblical texts and our ensuing conversations help us respond with greater faith and less fear in these situations?

OPTION: Based on the cover image, ask the group members to work together on a collage that reflects these thoughts on fear and faith, as well as their hopes for this group they will be part of over the next seven weeks. Post the collage and display it in the room throughout the course of the group meetings.

Blessing and Commissioning

Gather in a circle around or in front of the worship center. Invite closing thoughts from the participants on this session as well as looking ahead to the time to be shared together. Underscore that this series aims not only at the head, in terms of study and information, but also the heart, in terms of engaging ourselves in deeper trust of God. Affirm that such spiritual growth moves us inward by deepening our awareness of why we need not live afraid. It also moves us outward by encouraging us to put this trust into practice and action for the sake of the world God so loves.

Offer these or similar words for a blessing and commissioning:

Go with God's holy presence to assure you that you do not journey alone.

Go with Christ's gracious favor to remind you that God seeks your good and the good of all.

Go with Spirit's saving power to uphold, help, and strengthen you.

Go, and do not live afraid.

Session 1   Fear and Faith

To explore the dynamics of fear, faith, and love in our journey with God and others

Preparation

Cover a small table with colored cloths suggesting the hues of a rainbow. Place a candle on the table along with matches and/or lighter. Have adequate chairs and lighting for the size of group you expect. Also, for the "Entering the Theme" exercise, be prepared to rearrange chairs to allow access for participants to stand across the length of the room.

Materials needed: Bibles and copies of *Do Not Live Afraid* for each participant; lined paper and pens; art material that your group members will be comfortable using (marking pens, watercolors, chalk, and suitable paper to work on)

Gathering

Greet participants. Begin the session by inviting everyone to offer their name and a sentence or two stating reasons for being part of this group. Start with yourself.

Light the candle on the worship center. Offer a prayer that seeks God's leading in this meeting and throughout this study that will help the group not to live afraid.

Carry out the exercise suggested in the opening paragraph of chapter 1 (page 14). Designate one side of the room as "the fear of [God] is the beginning of wisdom" and the other as "perfect love casts out fear." Invite individuals to stand at or between those sides based on which reflects their core beliefs. Invite comments as to why individuals stand where they do.

Repeat this exercise, asking participants to move (or stay where they are) based on the following scenarios, and then to comment on why they stand where they do:

- You find out a loved one has been diagnosed with a terminal illness.
- You hear of a blatant act of aggression or terror in the world.

Reflect on ideas or questions this exercise may have raised.

Reflecting

Read Exodus 1:8-21. Ask and discuss: (1) What do we learn here about fear? (2) What do we learn here about faith? (3) What do we learn here about love and/or God? Read Proverbs 9:10 and 1 John 4:18-19. After each, discuss the preceding questions.

Invite participants to share with the group what from chapter 1 spoke most deeply to them, what reflected (or contradicted) their experiences or faith, and what questions the material raised. Use the sharing as a springboard into discussing issues and concerns that connect the material to the lives of the participants, your congregation, and the wider community and world. Suggest that participants also reflect on the four spiritual exercises. Ask which of the exercises brought some new insight or raised some question about their lives and spiritual journey. Again, encourage connections with issues and concerns for this day.

If you have a large group (over twelve persons), form small groups to carry out the preceding discussions, allowing individuals more time to speak. If you do form small groups, gather afterward as a whole group and have small groups report briefly.

Responding

Have participants create a journal entry or artwork that reflects on a fear they struggle with in their lives and/or faith. Use the following questions as guides for reflection:

- What is the nature and/or power of this fear? How might this chapter's biblical backgrounds speak to that fear?
- Where do you experience God in the midst of this fear?

Gather the group together. Invite any who wish to share something of their experience to do so. Respect the silence of those not comfortable sharing.

Engage the third spiritual exercise for this chapter as a group. Ask the participants to identify those they fear *for* in their community and acknowledge the threats. Choose one individual and/or group you can covenant to help. Determine what action you can realistically take.

Blessing and Commissioning

Invite adults to lift up what they have gained from this session. Encourage them to raise questions that may still linger. Make note of those as you plan future sessions.

Review the action the group has covenanted to take in the coming week, and relate how it connects the book's title of *Do Not Live Afraid* to this chapter's emphasis on the ethical dimension of our faith and spirituality. Gather the group in a circle around or in front of the worship center. Say these or similar words:

> **As God has gathered us in this session, so God now sends us as God's people to do the works of the Spirit, to live by the grace of Christ, and to trust that love, not fear, is God's ultimate word and promise to us and to all. Amen.**

Session 2   God's Presence, Favor, and Advocacy

To explore how God's presence, favor, and advocacy form the basis for not living afraid

Preparation

Cover a small table with colored cloths suggesting the hues of a rainbow. Place a candle on the table along with matches and/or lighter.

Materials needed: Bibles and copies of *Do Not Live Afraid*, hymnals or songbooks with song of choice, accompanist or a recording if you plan to sing it (unless you or another feels comfortable leading a cappella).

Gathering

Welcome the participants. Introduce any newcomers to the group. Light the candle. Sing or read the verses of a hymn or song that celebrates God's presence with us. Possibilities could include the following: "I Was There to Hear Your Borning Cry," "I Want Jesus to Walk with Me," "Kum Ba Yah," or another song traditionally used in your congregation.

Invite participants to recall an experience where they were grateful to have the presence and support of someone with them. Form groups of three. Give each person an opportunity to share his or her story and why that person's presence meant so much in that situation. Gather the group together. Have participants close their eyes, and recall an experience where they were especially grateful for *God's presence* in their lives. Raise the following for silent reflection:

- What fears may have lain in the background of that situation?

- How has that experience shaped your faith?

Lead the group in a prayer of thanks for God's presence in those times and in this time of community.

Reflecting

Form two groups. Assign Isaiah 41:10 to one group and Revelation 21:3-4 to the other. Have each group discuss: (1) what is the most surprising word or promise; why? (2) What is the most comforting word or promise; why? (3) What question(s) does this passage leave you with? Gather the groups together, and share summaries of the conversations around each of the three questions.

OPTION: Form groups and assign passages as described above. Explain that each group will develop a series of body sculptures and/or movements that illustrate its passage. Allow time for groups to plan. Ask the Isaiah group to present its series of movements. Invite the other group members to call out words or phrases they saw embodied. Have the Revelation group make its presentation; the other group members call out words or phrases they saw embodied. Afterward, discuss what was hardest to portray and what was recognized—and possible reasons for both.

Invite participants to share with the group what from chapter 2 spoke most deeply to them, what reflected (or contradicted) their experiences or faith, and what questions the material raised. Use the sharing as a springboard into discussing issues and concerns that connect the material to the lives of the participants, your congregation, and the wider community and world. Suggest that participants also reflect on the four spiritual exercises. Ask which of the exercises brought some new insight or raised some question about their lives and spiritual journey. Again, encourage connections with issues and concerns for this day.

If you have a large group (over twelve persons), form small groups to carry out the preceding discussions, allowing individuals more time to speak. If you do form small groups, gather afterward as a whole group and have small groups report briefly.

Responding

Re-form the earlier groups of three used during the GATHERING. Have the groups do Spiritual Exercise #2 from this chapter. Rather than silently reflecting after each time "I am your God" is spoken, share the responses to the questions listed in the exercise. Affirm that no one needs to share, particularly about fears, if he or she chooses not to and encourage the groups to respect that decision.

The passages from Isaiah and Revelation both speak to communities that face difficult times. Identify groups in your immediate community and the wider world that face such sadness and grief. Consider ways that you, as individuals and as a group, might become an advocate for them. It might be volunteering at a nearby nursing home, spending time with elders who are often forgotten. It might be offering to serve as a tutor, an adopted "grandparent," or a big brother or sister to children and youth who are at risk. It might involve your support of refugees or social justice ministry. Have individuals and/or small groups choose one of these—and if one can be undertaken by the whole group together, do that. Allow the promise of God's presence, favor, and advocacy to engage your group members in one or more new ministries of presence, favor, and advocacy as Christ's disciples.

Blessing and Commissioning

Invite adults to share what has been important to them in this session and what they will take from here. Encourage them to follow through with the advocacies decided upon in RESPONDING, and to consider ways to involve others in your community to do so.

Form a circle. Explain that the blessing will go around the circle. Turn to the person on your right, say his or her name followed by the words: **Do not be afraid; God is with you; God is for you.** That person turns to his or her right, repeats these words; this process continues until all have received blessing. Go over the words with the group and then begin the circle blessing.

Session 3   For the Sake of Trust

To explore how opening in trust to God bids us set fear aside

Preparation

Cover a small table with colored cloths suggesting the hues of a rainbow. Place a candle on the table along with matches and/or lighter.

Materials needed: Bibles and copies of *Do Not Live Afraid*; lined paper and pens for those who choose to journal.

Gathering

Welcome the participants. Introduce any newcomers to the group. Form a circle around or in front of the worship center. Light the candle. Explain that together you will craft an opening prayer of trust. First, ask members to consider a reason or experience that causes them to trust God. Then, go around the circle or gathering and invite those willing to do so to offer a sentence prayer that lifts up that reason or experience in thanks to God. Hold hands, and offer the prayers—with you as leader starting. Go around the circle to the left. Explain that if someone does not want to offer a prayer aloud he or she will squeeze the hand of the person to his or her left. When the "circle" of prayer returns to you, offer a closing to the prayer.

Continue to hold hands. Invite members to recall a person whom they trust deeply. Imagine that the hands they now hold are that person's. Call to mind and heart what created your trust for that one. Ask members to reflect silently on this question: **What does your trust in that person make possible for you?** Next, invite participants to recall one person who trusts them. Imagine that they now hold his or her hands. Ask them to reflect silently on these questions: **What has led that person to consider you trustworthy? How does that individual's trust in you affect you?**

Observe a time of silence. Afterward, invite participants to identify what they might have learned or had reinforced about trust in this exercise. Ask: **How do those learnings connect to our trust in God? How might they shed light on the role trust plays in setting fear aside?**

Reflecting

Have participants read silently Genesis 15:1-6 and Luke 1:26-38, looking for (1) a cause for fear; (2) a gift of God; and (3) an expression of trust. Briefly share examples found.

Invite participants to tell the group what from chapter 3 spoke most deeply to them, what reflected (or contradicted) their experiences or faith, and what questions the material raised. Use the sharing as a springboard into discussing issues and concerns that connect the material to the lives of the participants, your congregation, and the wider community and world. Suggest that participants also reflect on the four spiritual exercises. Ask which of the exercises brought some new insight or raised some question about their lives and spiritual journey. Again, encourage connections with issues and concerns for this day.

If you have a large group (over twelve persons), form small groups to carry out the preceding discussions, allowing individuals more time to speak. If you do form small groups, gather afterward as a whole group and have small groups report briefly.

Responding

Give individuals the choice to work on the following exercise alone or with a partner. Reread the wheelbarrow story that begins on page 41. Reflect and then journal (if working alone) or discuss with a partner: **When have you experienced trust in God as a** choice of "getting in" and taking a risk or watching from the sidelines? What was at stake; what fears were at play? Why did you choose as you did? How has that experience shaped your practice of trust?

Gather the group together. Discuss the ways in which your congregation nurtures trust in its members and what sort of trust is emphasized. Consider and discuss also how the church itself evidences (or contradicts) trust in its programs and ministries (and, dare I say it, the budget). For example, if a stranger to your church appeared one day and spent the week with your community, what would she learn of trusting and of trustworthiness? Out of that conversation, reflect on how that nurture and embodiment of trust on the part of the congregation might be improved. Focus on one or two ideas that seem especially needful at this point in time. How might you pass on these ideas not only to appropriate leaders and committees, but how might you incorporated them into the life of the group?

Blessing and Commissioning

Invite participants to reflect on what they have gained from this session by way of insights, encouragements, and/or questions that linger. Underscore that trust, as emphasized in the chapter's opening paragraphs, is foundational to relationship with God.

Recall the opening prayer used in GATHERING. All of those affirmations reflect on God's trustworthiness: trustworthiness we have experienced in our own lives, trustworthiness that serves as the basis for why we do not need to live afraid. God's love and grace can be trusted. Invite participants to join you in repeating that phrase three times as today's words of blessing and commissioning: *God's love and grace can be trusted.*

Session 4   For the Sake of Vocation

To explore how God's word not to be afraid calls us to the vocation of not living afraid

Preparation

Cover a small table with colored cloths suggesting the hues of a rainbow. Place a candle on the table along with matches and/or lighter.

Materials needed: Bibles and copies of *Do Not Live Afraid*, hymnals or songbooks with song of choice, an accompanist or a recording if you plan to sing it (unless you or another feel comfortable leading a cappella), lined paper and pens, arts and crafts materials

Gathering

Welcome the participants and introduce any newcomers. Form a circle around or in front of the worship center. Light the candle. Read or sing a hymn or from your tradition that lifts up God's call upon our lives. Possibilities could include the following: "Here I Am, Lord"; "Jesus Calls Us"; "Come, Labor On."

Ask members to recall an experience of being singled out to perform a task that took them by surprise. Have them call out a word or phrase that reflects their initial reaction to this surprising request. Next, ask them to consider the background factors that helped them determine their response. Ask them to call out a word or phrase that indicates what weighed in the direction of "thanks, but no thanks." Request that they call out a word or phrase that indicates what weighed in the direction of "yes, I will." Invite participants to speak briefly about how this experience connects to their understanding of call or vocation in faith.

Offer an opening prayer that seeks God's presence in the gathering and openness to God's invitation not to be afraid when we find ourselves called by God.

Reflecting

Read aloud Deuteronomy 31:7-8 and Luke 5:1-11 to the group. As you read, ask members to listen and make notes on these questions: (1) What causes for fear are at work here? (2) What directions could this fear take in the lives of these characters? (3) What "vocation" is at stake for these characters? After the reading, invite members to share their responses briefly. Ask: **Where do you see connections between these passages and contemporary issues of fear and vocation?**

Invite participants to share with the group what from chapter 4 spoke most deeply to them, what reflected (or contradicted) their experiences or faith, and what questions the material raised. Use the sharing as a springboard into discussing issues and concerns that connect the material to the lives of the participants, your congregation, and the wider community and world. Suggest that participants also reflect on the four spiritual exercises. Ask which of the exercises brought some new insight or raised some question about their lives and spiritual journey. Again, encourage connections with issues and concerns for this day.

If you have a large group (over twelve persons), form small groups to carry out the preceding discussions, allowing individuals more time to speak. If you do form small groups, gather afterward as a whole group and have small groups report briefly.

Responding

Have individuals turn to the paragraph on page 57 that begins: "Imagine also your setting aside the fears that typically get in your way." After all have read it silently, suggest that participants create an expression of their answer to "From now on you will. . . ." It could be a poem, journal entry, or a craft work creation. Encourage adults to be creative as they consider what is asked in that paragraph and as they respond in this activity. Afterward, allow time for those who wish to tell about their creation to do so.

Talk about the meaning of vocation in the context of your wider community and the world. Ask: **Where do these passages and this chapter lead us, as individuals and as church, to see our vocation connected to pressing human and environmental needs around us? What fears might otherwise hold us back?** Focus on one particular calling to ministry or service your church "owns." In what ways might this session enable the group members to support and even participate in that calling in deeper ways and/or encourage others not to fear participating? Covenant to do so as persons are able.

Blessing and Commissioning

Gather in a circle around or in front of the worship center. Give individuals an opportunity to reflect, silently and/or aloud, on this session's connection to their lives, in particular to their sense of vocation and God's invitation to practice that vocation without fear. Affirm the responses of those who speak and the thoughts of those who choose not to.

Close by having each person step into the center of the circle and receive these words of blessing and commissioning adapted from this session's biblical texts: **(Name), do not be afraid; be strong and bold, for you are the one God calls.** Practice saying this several times so the group is comfortable with it. Then, offer it together to each person as he or she stands, one at a time, in the center of the circle.

Session 5   For the Sake of Witness

To explore how setting fear aside opens the way for and is itself an act of witness

Preparation

Cover a small table with colored cloths suggesting the hues of a rainbow. Place a candle on the table along with matches and/or lighter.

Materials needed: Bibles and copies of *Do Not Live Afraid*, copy(ies) of "How Can I Keep from Singing" ("My Life Flows On")

Gathering

Welcome the participants. Introduce any newcomers. Make a circle around or in front of the worship center. Light the candle. Ask someone to read Romans 10:14-15 from the New Revised Standard Version. If participants have other translations of those verses, read them as well. Offer a prayer that thanks God for those from whom we have heard faith's word in the past and that seeks God's guidance in this session in exploring what it means for us to be faith's witnesses for others.

Ask the group members find a partner and then turn to Spiritual Exercise #1 (page 71). Carry out the "elevator conversation" in pairs. Each person will take a turn as the one who asks the "why do you bother with all this religion stuff" *and* the one who has thirty seconds to respond. Allow participants time to gather their thoughts to respond. Carry out the activity. Afterward, invite participants to reflect on the experience: what they may have learned or been surprised by, either in another's response or their own.

Reflecting

Form two groups. Assign Jeremiah 1:4-10 to one and Matthew 28:8-10 to the other. Have each group read its passage and come up with one-sentence answers to these questions: (1) What does this passage reveal about what it means to be a witness? (2) What does this passage hint at fears that stand in the way of witness and how God makes witness possible? (3) How do those previous questions and answers connect to what it means to be a witness today? Gather the groups together. Share and then discuss responses to the questions (do one question at a time).

Invite participants to share with the group what from chapter 5 spoke most deeply to them, what reflected (or contradicted) their experiences or faith, and what questions the material raised. Use the sharing as a springboard into discussing issues and concerns that connect the material to the lives of the participants, your congregation, and the wider community and world. Suggest that participants also reflect on the four spiritual exercises. Ask which of the exercises brought some new insight or raised some question about their lives and spiritual journey. Again, encourage connections with issues and concerns for this day.

If you have a large group (over twelve persons), form small groups to carry out the preceding discussions, allowing individuals more time to speak. If you do form small groups, gather afterward as a whole group and have small groups report briefly.

Responding

Invite the group to reread Spiritual Exercise #4 (page 72). Brainstorm concerns and issues that need the witness of faith in the wider community and in the world. Focus on one that resonates with your group not only in its importance but one that you together can address in some way. Use the two questions in the exercise to focus your conversation: (1) What word and/or action of witness seems most needed, most timely, to you? (2) What part might you play in bringing that witness to bear, alone or with others? Determine what you can and will do together in the coming week(s) to carry out that witness.

OPTION: Do a continuum exercise. Designate one side of the meeting space as "I am completely comfortable witnessing to my faith to another person." Designate the other side of the meeting space as "I am very uncomfortable witnessing to my faith to another person." Invite participants to stand at either side or points in between based on their experience. Ask individuals to state why they stand where they do. What fears are involved? How have they experienced strength or encouragement to do so? Repeat the exercise, with the change of witnessing to groups rather than another individual. Do the same sharing, and raise the same questions for discussion. Afterward, ask participants to consider ways in which the congregation might help individuals grow more comfortable and effective as witnesses.

Blessing and Commissioning

Gather the group around or in front of the worship center. Invite responses, comments, and/or questions that arise out of this session. Ask: **What do you understand or see in a new way about witness and its connection to not living afraid?**

Close by reading (in unison, if possible) the hymn/poem: "How Can I Keep from Singing" ("My Life Flows On"). Invite participants to hear (speak) it as an affirmation and a commissioning of their own witness.

Session 6   For the Sake of Justice

To explore how God's imperative for our doing what is just and right relies on setting fear aside

Preparation

Cover a small table with colored cloths suggesting the hues of a rainbow. Place a candle on the table along with matches and/or lighter.

Materials needed: Bibles and copies of *Do Not Live Afraid*, music for "Once to Every Man and Nation" (if group is unfamiliar with the tune EBENEZER / TON-Y-BOTEL, you may want to say the two verses together. If you want to sing it, consider playing the song as the group gathers and then practice it before the session begins).

Gathering

Welcome the participants. Introduce any newcomers. Make a circle around or in front of the worship center. Light the candle. Invite the group to "pray" Psalm 146. Explain that you will read the psalm aloud one verse at a time, pausing twenty seconds between verses. In the break between verses, invite individuals to offer prayers evoked by that verse.

Ask participants to recall a situation where someone or some group in your church or wider community acted upon an issue of justice that was controversial at the time. Reflect on: what motivated their decision and action; what made their stand controversial; what fears played a role in the situation as it unfolded? In pairs, have persons share their responses. Gather the whole group. Ask: **As you listened and spoke to each other, what connections did you make between doing justice and facing fears?**

Reflecting

Ask two volunteers to read aloud Zechariah 8:11-17 and 1 Peter 3:13-17. Instruct the group to listen to both passages with these questions in mind: (1) What constitutes the doing of justice here? (2) Why might such doing of justice need the assurance of "do not be afraid" or "do not fear" given in these passages? After the readings, discuss these questions and invite other comments from the participants about the relationships among faith, justice, and fear.

Invite participants to share with the group what from chapter 6 spoke most deeply to them, what reflected (or contradicted) their experiences or faith, and what questions the material raised. Use the sharing as a springboard into discussing issues and concerns that connect the material to the lives of the participants, your congregation, and the wider community and world. Suggest that participants also reflect on the four spiritual exercises. Ask which of the exercises brought some new insight or raised some question about their lives and spiritual journey. Again, encourage connections with issues and concerns for this day.

If you have a large group (over twelve persons), form small groups to carry out the preceding discussions, allowing individuals more time to speak. If you do form small groups, gather afterward as a whole group and have small groups report briefly.

Responding

Read aloud the theme for today's session: **to explore how God's imperative for our doing what is just and right relies on setting fear aside.** Suggest that participants record on paper or in their journals responses to the following questions: (1) What one issue of justice do you have passion for, and why? (2) What fear(s) compromises your expression of that passion for justice in action? (3) How might this chapter's reading and this session encourage you to set this fear aside?

Having considered setting fear aside for the sake of doing justice on a personal level, invite the group to consider God's call to do justice in terms of collective concern and action. As a group work through Spiritual Exercise #3 (pages 83–84) from this chapter. Encourage participants to focus on one individual or group for whom justice has been denied and upon one action they together can take this week, as well as what each can do individually. Covenant together to carry through on these actions.

Blessing and Commissioning

Gather the group around or in front of the worship center. Invite participants to offer responses to this session: insights that have come to them, questions that still linger, reinforcements of truths that relate to God's imperative to do justice and God's gift of not fearing to do so. Sing or say in unison the two verses of "Once to Every Man and Nation" (page 73; see suggestion, PREPARATION).

Offer the group the following commissioning to do justice (adapted from Zechariah 8:16-17 and Amos 5:24):

These are the things that you shall do:
   speak the truth to one another;
   render in your gates judgments that are true
      and that make for peace;
   do not devise evil in your hearts against one another;
   love no false oath; and
   let justice roll down like waters and
      righteousness like an ever-flowing stream.

Session 7   For the Sake of Transformation

To explore how setting aside fear opens us to transformation by the hands of God

Preparation

Cover a small table with colored cloths suggesting the hues of a rainbow. Place a candle on the table along with matches and/or lighter.

Materials needed: Bibles, newsprint, and copies of *Do Not Live Afraid*, a copy of "The Touch of the Master's Hand" (readily available online), lined paper and pens

Gathering

Welcome the participants. Introduce any newcomers to the group. Form a circle with chairs around or in front of the worship center. When all participants are seated, light the candle. Offer a prayer inviting God's presence in this gathering, and praying for openness to the work of God's Spirit among and within us during this time. Read, or ask one of the participants who is good at dramatic reading to read the poem "The Touch of the Master's Hand."

Invite adults to close their eyes and recall an experience where they found healing and strength through another's touch. Ask: **What was it that made that touch so important to you? . . . In what ways did that touch dispel some fear in that moment? . . . In what ways did it transform the situation you were in and perhaps even you? . . .** Ask participants to open their eyes and be at peace. Invite any who are willing to share briefly what they carry with them from that experience.

Reflecting

Form two groups. Assign Genesis 50:15-21 to one group and Matthew 17:1-7 to the other group. Have groups read and discuss their passages with these questions in mind: (1) What or who is transformed in this story? (2) What fears stand in the way of or result from such change in this passage? (3) What does this story reveal about transformation, then and now. Gather the groups together, and have a spokesperson for each group report briefly on its discussion.

Invite participants to share with the group what from chapter 7 spoke most deeply to them, what reflected (or contradicted) their experiences or faith, and what questions the material raised. Use the sharing as a springboard into discussing issues and concerns that connect the material to the lives of the participants, your congregation, and the wider community and world. Suggest that participants also reflect on the four spiritual exercises. Ask which of the exercises brought some new insight or raised some question about their lives and spiritual journey. Again, encourage connections with issues and concerns for this day.

If you have a large group (over twelve persons), form small groups to carry out the preceding discussions, allowing individuals more time to speak. If you do form small groups, gather afterward as a whole group and have small groups report briefly.

Responding

Have participants consider the "cutting edge" for transformation in their lives. In what one area of life do they see the need for transformation most greatly—and experience the struggle or fear of such change with equal intensity? Invite participants to write a prayer that seeks God's help and transformation in their lives. Encourage participants at the end to offer this prayer every morning and every evening of the coming week with an open spirit.

Invite the group to brainstorm aspects of church life, their wider community, and the world where transformation is greatly needed—and greatly feared. Write these on newsprint. Have the group determine one priority for such change in church, in community, in world. Work together, or form three working groups (one for each setting), to identify ways in which we might open ourselves to God's work of transformation in those areas—and to consider what fear may need to be set aside. Remembering that this is the final session of the study, identify ways the group might continue to work for such change, as individuals and with others, as we set fear aside and open ourselves and those situations to God's transformation.

Blessing and Commissioning

Gather the group around or in front of the worship center. Invite responses, comments, and/or questions that arise out of this session. Since this is the final gathering for study, invite participants to reflect and comment on this experience, both in terms of the material covered and the group life shared. Thank them for their participation and for the ways they have opened themselves through this study to God's transformation.

Form a circle, holding hands. Encourage participants to feel the touch of those persons beside whom they stand. God in Christ touches our lives for the sake of healing and with the gift of strengthening, so that we need not live afraid but rather by trust and through love. Going around the circle, encourage participants offer a sentence prayer in thanks, in hope, in trust of God and/or this community. Close the prayer by saying aloud the final words of chapter 7: **So do not be afraid: of God, of the future, of our transformation in Christ. What God seeks is our good. What God offers is love incarnate. Trust these things—and do not live afraid!**

notes

1. Joanna Bourke, *Fear: A Cultural History* (Emeryville, CA: Shoemaker and Hoard/Avalon Publishing Group, 2006), x.

2. Billy Graham, "Faith," in Clyde E. Fant Jr. and William M. Pinson Jr., eds., *Marshall to King*, vol. 12, *20 Centuries of Great Preaching* (Waco, TX: Word Books, 1971), 335.

3. John Indermark, *Setting the Christmas Stage: Readings for the Advent Season* (Nashville, TN: Upper Room Books, 2001), 81.

4. Richard Roberts, *The Renascence of Faith* (New York: Fleming H. Revell, 1912), 102.

5. James Russell Lowell, "Once to Every Man and Nation," *The Hymnal* (Saint Louis, MO: Eden Publishing House, 1941), no. 399.

about the author

JOHN INDERMARK lives in Naselle, Washington, with his wife, Judy, an E-911 dispatcher. Ordained in the United Church of Christ, John served as a parish pastor for sixteen years before being led to a ministry of writing that is now his full-time vocation. This book joins several others published by Upper Room Books. In addition, John writes Christian education curricula for *Seasons of the Spirit, The Present Word, New International Lectionary Annual,* and *Great Themes of the Bible.* He has published articles in *The Clergy Journal and Exchange* (a publication of the United Church of Canada).

In their spare time, John and Judy enjoy walking the area's logging roads and trails, puttering in the garden, and collecting rocks on the British Columbia coast and in the desert Southwest.